Alan Flusser

Author of
Clothes and The Man

Clothes and the Man

CLOTHES AND THE MAN

The Principles of Fine Men's Dress

Alan Flusser

Villard Books ■ New York 1989

Library of Congress Cataloging in Publication Data
Flusser, Alan J.
    Clothes and the man.
    1. Men's clothing.   I. Title.
TT618.F58   1985   646'.32   85-40191
ISBN 0-394-54623-7

Grateful acknowledgment is made to the following for permission to reprint previously
published material:
The Bettmann Archive: Photographs on pages 2,22 and 94.
Condé Nast Publications Inc.: Illustrations from *Apparel Arts* on pages 11, 12, 13,
14, 15, 16, 17, and 18. Copyright 1928, 1934, 1935, 1936, 1938 by The Condé
Nast Publications Inc. Copyright renewed 1956, 1962, 1963, 1964, 1966 by The
Condé Nast Publications Inc. Used by permission.
Culver Pictures: Photographs on pages 10 and 122.
Hartmarx Corporation: Ilustrations on pages 19, 20, and 21.
Phototeque: Photographs on pages x and 24.

Manufactured in Italy
9 8 7 6

To the women in my life:
Marilise, Janet, Rita, Skye, and Piper,
all of whom I love dearly,
none of whom I'd send to buy me a tie.

Author's Note

     With the publication of my first book, *Making the Man*, I thought I had answered most of the questions men asked about dressing. However, instead of satisfying men's curiosity, it seems that the book stimulated them to want to know more. As I toured around the country, I was repeatedly approached by men wanting to hear about the specifics of fine dress. For example, should a short man wear a double-breasted jacket? What style of shirt collar should a man with a long neck wear? What are the appropriate shoe styles for business wear? And so on. Thus my decision to write *Clothes and the Man*.

     Some of the ideas and statements included here were first expressed in my earlier book; much of what I said five years ago I saw no reason to change. Classic dressing is not a topical subject. It is about longevity and endurance. My hope is that this book will give men the knowledge to dress not only with style but with confidence.

Acknowledgments

There are a number of individuals who made significant contributions to the production of this book. The photography of Jane Corbett and the illustrations of Roland Descombes capture exactly the spirit I had in mind when I began this book. Their dedication to detail and unflagging enthusiasm made it a pleasure to work with them. Charles Salzberg aided me in my research and helped me focus my thoughts; I will always admire his perseverance and determination to "get it right." My brother Martin was an invaluable adviser. Few people combine his knowledge of clothing with an equal expertise in writing, both of which he unselfishly allowed me to share. The time spent together was another fine opportunity to renew our affectionate sibling rivalry. David Larkin brought his own love of clothes and highly developed craft to the task of designing this book. Linda Rosenberg performed the drudging but necessary service of turning my copy into readable, understandable prose. Todd Optican, my assistant, was always there when I needed him. And finally, Marc Jaffe, who is a special man to work with and to know. He understood the nature of this project from the beginning and refused to confine my ambitions for it.

The following individuals deserve special mention, each of whom contributed time and interest so that this book could come about.

Arthur Cooper—editor-in-chief, *Gentlemen's Quarterly*
Michael F. Coady—senior vice-president, Fairchild Publications
Cliff Grodd—president, Paul Stuart
Charles Rosner—friend and supporter
Stanley R. Jaffe—senior vice-president and general manager, Brooks Brothers
Mildred Schlesinger—advertising director, Brooks Brothers
Burton Berinsky—president, J. Lord Hatter Ltd.
Ron DiGennaro—fashion news editor, *Gentlemen's Quarterly*
Robert Beauchamp—executive editor, *Gentlemen's Quarterly*
Robert Gilotte—friend and sartorial conscience
Tom Davis—sales associate, Brooks Brothers
Charles Davidson—The Andover Shop
Allan Ellinger—friend and partner
Richard Merkin—a fine "dandy" friend
Denis Halbray—Anderson & Sheppard Ltd.
Norman Halsey—Anderson & Sheppard Ltd.
John Hitchcock—Anderson & Sheppard Ltd.
A. Careceni—Careceni, Milan
Alan Butler—Holiday & Brown Ltd.
Edward Tucker—Bowring & Arundel Ltd.
John Tucker—Bowring & Arundel Ltd.
Adrienne P. Williams—vice-president and pal, Alan Flusser Inc.
Irving E. Press—president, J. Press Inc.
Marta Fredricks—fashion news associate, *Gentlemen's Quarterly*
David Russo—director of publicity, Paul Stuart
Alan White—White, New Haven
Wolfgang Herzfeld—H. Herzfeld, New York

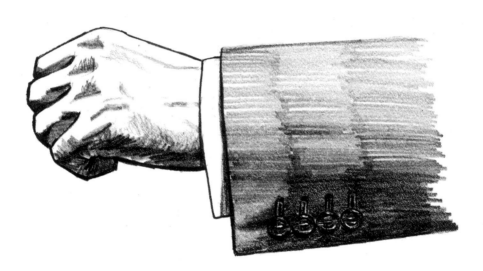

Contents

CARY GRANT—*One of the world's most elegant men. A pin collar on a fine-quality dress shirt paired with a solid satin tie, all in monochromatic colorations, are hallmarks of this man's individual style.*

Introduction

"Costly thy habit as thy purse can buy,
But not express'd in fancy; rich, not gaudy;
For the apparel oft proclaims the man."

—Polonius to Laertes,
HAMLET, Act I, Scene III

Cary Grant has a large head, but chances are you've never noticed. That's because Cary Grant understands how to dress appropriately, not only for the occasion at hand, but with a keen eye toward his own particular physique. Thus, instead of suits with natural shoulders, which would only accentuate the size of his head, he wears only those with wider shoulders, which create the illusion of his head being somewhat smaller than it actually is.

Unfortunately, this kind of stylistic acumen is not shared by the majority of American men. All too often they confuse dressing "fashionably" with dressing well. Fashion, as the word suggests, is fleeting. Nor is there any guarantee that someone dressing in the latest fashion is dressing well. Indeed, it is quite possible to wear all the latest things, from shoe to hat, and still look distinctly unstylish. Dressing well means selecting the clothes best suited to you, to make sure they fit and to wear them properly. And, finally, to give them your own personal touch.

Because the cost of good-quality clothing is high and will continue to rise, the purchase of a wardrobe can turn into a major expenditure. Certainly you wouldn't knowingly invest in something that's going to depreciate in value, so why buy clothing that you might wear no more than a few times? Isn't it far wiser to buy clothes you're likely to have around for many years, a wardrobe that will stand the test of time, leaving you in good stead regardless of how fashion changes? And if you purchase your clothing with an eye toward dressing well, discarding items becomes a matter of personal choice rather than a necessity due to outmoded styling.

Although it may in some cases border on the serious, lack of style or good taste is a problem that is far from hopeless. Rather, it is a problem that may be remedied simply through the education of the wearer.

Few are born with an innate sense of style, taste, and the knowledge of what looks good. Like almost everything else, a sense of style is acquired, but only through interest, exposure, and the application of experience, all of which may be derived from the careful observation of certain basic rules and principles of good taste.

I received my first lessons on how to dress from my father, for whom the possibilities of dressing well elicited considerable interest and enjoyment. He was in the real estate business, and he used the way he dressed to project a successful image. Many mornings I'd watch him go through his daily ritual of dressing for work. The shirt, the tie, the suit, the shoes were all carefully selected so that he looked and felt his best. I believed it was normal to take that much care in deciding how one should look, to put such thought into the appropriateness of the clothes he wore. I didn't realize then that my father was in a small minority of men, holdovers from a previous era, who not only appreciated the feel and look of fine clothing but respected the rules of taste and decorum.

Thus, in short, the ultimate aim of this book is to try to educate the reader about the basic principles of fine dressing. But what are the advantages of dressing well? Why should one even bother?

As it happens, the advantages are many. First of all, dress is a legitimate form of communication. As Pearl Binder noted in her book *The Peacock's Tail*, "Dress is the outward expression of man's state of mind, and it is his attire that tells the world what he thinks of himself." Clothes speak for us, whether we are aware of it or not. As Oscar E. Schoeffler, the long-time fashion editor of *Esquire*, warned, "Never underestimate the power of what you wear. . . . After all, there's just a small bit of you-yourself sticking out, at the cuff and at the neck. The rest of what the world sees is what you hang on the frame."

But there are other practical reasons for knowing the basics of dressing well. Whether by nature or conditioning, men do not like to shop. It is frequently a tedious and time-consuming process, something most men wish to do quickly and efficiently. However, the process can be made far easier if you know what to ask and look for. For instance, when you go into a store to buy a suit, the salesman might tell you that this year the trouser style is fuller. But if you have a small foot, you'd know that in order for you to look your best the trousers need to be less full, so that your feet are not swallowed up in a tidal wave of material.

Also, dressing is an activity that you perform every day. It takes a certain amount of time to button up your shirt and knot your tie, so why not make it an activity from which you can derive satisfaction?

This book will show you how to get that satisfaction. Basically, dressing is like any other skill. It takes knowledge and a certain amount of practice. The relationships and principles discussed in this book are not new. They were developed in the 1930s and for many years were handed down from father to son and from tailor to client. Then, starting in the 1960s, communication broke down. Young people stopped listening to what others, older than they, had to say, and a whole body of knowledge was almost lost. Now that people are once again interested in the way they dress, it is time to renew this communication.

The principles enumerated here are not meant to make all men dress alike. I, for one, loathe conformity. In fact, I admire the idiosyncratic or unpredictable dresser, the man who wears the odd shirt with the odd tie. I believe that you should do what's proper and then make it your own. And making it your own means that you ought to develop enough confidence to rely on your personal taste rather than on the dictates of a designer, store, or magazine. In this age of automation, dressing is one of the few areas left in life that is still under your control.

So why not do it with style?

Clothes and the Man

THE DUKE OF WINDSOR—*His influence on fashion in the
twentieth century was greater than that of Beau Brummell in the
nineteenth century.*

I

The 1930s:
The Height of Elegance

"Trust not the heart of that man for whom
old clothes are not venerable."
— *THOMAS CARLYLE*

American designers of men's clothes have in recent years looked to
the past for inspiration in creating their new collections. No era has
been overlooked. They have recycled baggy topcoats from the fifties,
wide-shouldered suits and surplus wear from the forties. But
perhaps no era has been more fruitful as a source of inspiration than
the 1930s. This was a time when the American taste level was at its
height, the elegance of our clothing equal to that of any European
country. In fact, the thirties could really be considered the time
when the American style of dress reached its pinnacle, a period
when a good many men were properly concerned with the clothes
they wore and the image they projected. It was an era during which
the foundations of good taste in men's wear were laid—foundations
and relationships that still apply today.

This era of fine dress did not occur spontaneously. On the
contrary, it was the result of a number of factors, all of which
converged in the late 1920s and early '30s. There was, for
instance, the new prosperity of the postwar years, which enabled
Americans to spend more money on clothing as well as affording
them the leisure time to travel throughout Europe, where they
were exposed to a different style of dress.

In the early part of this century, men's clothing was predominantly utilitarian and rather unimaginative. World War I changed all this, as men began to shake off the effects of the Victorian influence, which had hidden the body under yards of cloth. Servicemen returning from the war found that they enjoyed the comfort and functionality of their uniforms and would now settle for nothing less in their day-to-day business clothes.

They didn't have to. Americans had more money now as business boomed. More money allowed them to travel, to broaden their horizons, and many crossed the Atlantic to England and France. Naturally, when they returned, they brought back with them suitcases filled with the latest fashions being worn on the Continent. This was especially true of college students who were traveling abroad. Quick to become fashion-conscious, they had little trouble finding inspiration at Oxford University, where students had taken to wearing wide-bottom trousers, natural-shoulder jackets, button-down shirts with regimental ties, and colorful argyle socks, all of which were brought back and absorbed into the American college wardrobe.

Ultimately, it was the English style of dress that caught the fancy of American men, and no one represented this style better than the then Prince of Wales, who was later to become Edward VIII and then the Duke of Windsor. Unquestionably, no one in the world exerted more influence on the way men dressed than did the suave and elegant prince, whose personal style of dress was exposed to the world through newsreels, newspapers, and magazines. Americans have always had a fondness for royalty, and the dashing prince, who loved publicity, was ready to oblige. As someone once remarked, "If there hadn't been a Prince of Wales, someone in the menswear industry would have had to invent him."

When the prince wore a particular garment in a particularly idiosyncratic way, he bestowed upon it his personal imprimatur, thus making it not only possible but highly desirable for others to wear it as well. Clothing-industry advertising even traded shame-lessly on his name by proclaiming in their ads "As worn by the Prince."

His influence was legendary. Unofficially England's

"Ambassador of Good Will," the prince appeared one day at Belmont Park, on Long Island, wearing a Panama hat; with more than fifty thousand others present, he thus revived this style of chapeau at a time when it was decidedly out of fashion. On another occasion, he was the only man to attend a polo match in Meadow Brook, Long Island, wearing brown buckskin shoes along with a chalk-striped flannel suit. This heretofore unheard-of style innovation resulted the next year in hundreds of those in attendance appearing with brown shoes on their feet.

The prince was also responsible for the popularity of the tab collar, the Windsor knot, the double-breasted jacket with long roll lapel (known as the Kent, for his brother, though the prince wore it first and allowed his sibling to receive credit for the innovation), and the re-emergence of the Fair Isle Shetland sweater.

Though today the word "fashion" has a somewhat questionable connotation, in the late twenties and throughout the thirties the notion of being "in fashion" was most desirable. Hence, the American man paid close attention to what was being worn by the style setters. Nowhere could he receive a better lesson in how to dress properly than by watching the images being projected on the silver screen.

By the time the decade of the thirties arrived, the economic bubble had burst as the Depression set in. Now, with matters so tenuous in the real world, Americans in increasing numbers turned to the movies to provide them with an escape. Men as well as women flocked to movie theaters, where they watched film stars such as Fred Astaire, Clark Gable, Cary Grant, Adolphe Menjou, Gary Cooper, and the Fairbankses, Sr. and Jr., impeccably dressed in the most up-to-date fashions, parade fifty feet high in front of them. These film stars joined others whose photographs flooded newspapers and magazines—the Prince of Wales, of course, and the Duke of Kent, the writer Lucius Beebe, and socialite Anthony J. Drexel Biddle, Jr.—arbiters of style. Finally American men had role models at home to whom they could look in order to "learn" how to dress properly.

And look they did. The interest was certainly there; men

wanted to know how to dress with style and flair. They wanted to look their best. Taking advantage of this newfound interest in dressing well, *Apparel Arts*, the forerunner of *Gentlemen's Quarterly*, first appeared in 1921 and was eagerly seized upon by men's clothing stores, who used it as a counter catalog. Then, in the fall of 1933, in the depths of the Depression, another new men's magazine, *Esquire*, appeared on the newsstands. This new periodical made the salient point that although the country as a whole might be in dire straits, there were still plenty of people who enjoyed reading about what the minority unaffected by the Depression was wearing and how they were living. Ironically, then, the Depression "returned fashion to the hands of those who could still afford it," as noted by *Esquire's Encyclopedia of Twentieth-Century Men's Fashions*. "The look was decidedly British, for the rich American of the thirties was the same man who had shopped Savile Row in the twenties."

All these elements came together in the thirties. By then, American men had, by dint of their exposure to fine clothing via the Prince of Wales, movies, and their own travel throughout Europe, formulated certain basic principles of dress that would prove enduring. As the designer Yves Saint-Laurent recently observed, "By 1930 to '36 a handful of basic shapes were created that still prevail today as a sort of scale of expression, with which every man can project his own personality and style."

What were these principles and shapes? To begin with, American men realized that clothing should not be worn to hide the natural lines of the body, but, rather, to conform to them, thereby enhancing the male physique. At the same time, clothes should not be too obvious. Instead, they had to become part of the man who was wearing them. The idea of clothing was not to set the man apart (as had been the case for centuries, when kings and noblemen dressed primarily to accomplish just that) but to allow him to be an individual among individuals.

After years of concealing the body under bulky, austere clothing and then a decade of experimentation which included suits that exaggerated the lines of the body, Americans had finally learned that clothing had to flatter rather than be conspicuous.

But there was another criterion as well: clothes had to be comfortable. Though they need not actually be old and worn, they had to fit as though they were, which, to the American man of the thirties, meant that clothing had to conform to his own body. The ideal was that clothes ought to be part of the man, not the other way around. For someone like Fred Astaire, this was reflected in his habit of taking a few twirls around his tailor's shop to make sure his new suit fit properly, that it was roomy enough for him to feel comfortable in.

During this period, an entirely new vocabulary concerning men's clothes was developed out of the collaboration of the custom tailor and his knowing clients. This body of knowledge governing the shape and proper proportions of clothing details such as lapels, collars, trouser length and width, and shoe styles still applies to fine dressing today.

Additionally, there were very definite rules of propriety. One dressed in a certain manner for a particular occasion. As a result, it was during the thirties that the sportswear industry suddenly burgeoned. It would have been inappropriate to appear in a casual setting wearing business clothes, and so appropriate sportswear had to be developed.

As *Apparel Arts* once noted, the thirties were a time when "the average fellow was light in the wallet, but heavier on leisure time." This leisure time was spent in dress-up sportswear—namely, sports jackets, hats, ties, shirts, and slacks. Prior to the 1930s, there had been only two major seasons in the menswear industry: fall and spring. But now a summer season, represented by linen, seersucker, Palm Beach cloth, and other washable fabrics, was added. Also, color began to play a major role, as a wider selection was made available, with a particular emphasis placed on pastels. Sportswear came to reflect a casual comfort and thus adhered to the strict principles already promulgated for business wear.

Thus, by the mid-thirties, the American male was the picture of elegance. His clothes were finely made. He respected rules of propriety and yet, with imagination, he was also able to project a sense of individual elegance. Is it any wonder, then, that the 1930s marked the peak of stylish dress in America? It was the height of elegance, a period that offered just the proper balance in dress, with a relationship not so much to fashion as simply to what looked and felt best on a man's body.

Since the end of World War II, American men have strayed from the high standards and basic principles of fine dress established in the thirties. In some respects, this was an understandable result of the changes in the way Americans worked and the loss of formality in everyday life. With the precipitous rise in the price of custom tailoring, leadership in the menswear industry devolved into the hands of the mass manufacturers. They in turn attempted to boost sales by offering changes in clothing in order to entice people to buy more—though not necessarily more flattering—styles. This was not unlike the efforts of the American automobile manufacturers, who learned that by altering car designs each year they could stimulate sales.

At the same time, the individual's taste level was also being challenged by magazines offering the latest styles. One of the choices was the so-called bold look, introduced by *Esquire* in 1948. This utterly contrived look leaned heavily on matched accessories such as ties and handkerchiefs in sharp contrast to the sophisticated, serendipitous style of the 1930s.

The 1950s were the Age of Conformity. Young men returning from the service were anxious to fit right in with the Establishment. One of the quickest and most efficient ways to do this was to dress as the Establishment did, which meant donning the "Ivy League" look. Now, instead of trying to look like themselves, everyone was trying to look like the next person while wearing the boxlike sack suit. Of course, manufacturers were perfectly happy with this state of affairs, as it was a boon for them. With one silhouette to fit many different physiques, they were able to boost their profits while holding down their overhead.

An important event that promised to have a large impact on the way men dressed was the introduction in the mid-fifties of man-made fabrics, including rayon and nylon. These fibers led to the creation of blends that extended the wearability of suits by making them washable. Taking this a step further, the development of the so-called miracle fabrics—synthetic fibers that included Dacron, Dynel, and Vicara—allowed suits to be lightweight, spot-resistant, crease-resistant, able to hold a press, and durable. Unfortunately, the technology was so limited that only the most unsophisticated of designs could be manufactured. Realizing this, fabric producers created new looks such as synthetic texturizing, doubleknits, and so on. The choice for the American man buying a popular-priced suit went from bad to worse.

The 1960s were a decade of unrest, of rebellion against the Establishment, and the conservatism of the 1950s. Certainly this rebellion was reflected in the clothing Americans wore, as the youth of this country became far more concerned with self-expression than with classical style. The idea was to leave the crowd, not join it, and the clothing industry made this simple by introducing a plethora of choices. Now all the extremes in clothing styles, from the Nehru jacket and Edwardian suit to flared and bell-bottom trousers, were considered and worn.

Perhaps the most disquieting element of dress during this period was a shocking case of role reversal. Whereas in the past the knowledge of how to dress was handed down from father to son, now all that seemed to change. Suddenly it was the father who was looking to his son for instruction on how to dress. For perhaps the first time in history, it was the youth who were dictating styles. Grown men wanted to look young at any cost, and the predictable result was the further deterioration of the 1930s' legacy of elegant dress.

Today American men are finally beginning to learn from the mistakes of the past, many of which still hang in their closets. They have, in a sense, become educated at their own expense. They are more thoughtful in their choices now because the cost of clothing is so high. They are also more knowledgeable about what they purchase. And the menswear industry has responded accordingly. Like the American automobile industry, it too has learned from its mistakes. Just as Detroit has begun to engineer car models along simple, functional lines, the clothing industry has done much the same. Most of the extreme styles have been eliminated, and the notion of quality is returning to menswear.

Naturally, throughout the years following the 1930s there have always remained a small but confident group of knowledgeable dressers who refused to be swayed by the fashions of the moment. Their example is worth noting. The 1930s established an unparalleled standard of elegance and style, against which we would do well to measure our own current efforts.

Culver Pictures

Culver Pictures

ANTHONY J. DREXEL BIDDLE, JR.
—*Scion of one of America's wealthiest and most socially prominent families, he epitomized the American elegance of the 1930s. Many considered him the best-dressed man in America.*

from Apparel Arts, January–February 1938, vol. viii, no. iii

*Central Park,
New York City*

Against the background of an old hansom cab stand near New York's Plaza Hotel, the classic yet sporty clothes of the mid-1930s, as exemplified by these two men, display a quiet elegance. They are correctly dressed in clothing that reflects the semi-sports trend—for example, the black mohair pullover worn by the man on the right substitutes for a waistcoat. The other man's light-colored raincoat has comfortable raglan shoulders—a style that derives from the English hunting coat, which has a somewhat longer and fuller skirt. In fact, England is also the major influence on the suit worn by the first man: marine blue as a stylish color for men originated in London, and it is used here in a flannel suit that is striped with pearl gray. The lapel of the four-button double-breasted jacket has been rolled to the bottom button by the wearer, but it could also be buttoned at the top. The jacket has piped pockets and a plain back, but side vents would have been just as appropriate. The comfort and easy fit across the chest and shoulders are characteristics of the British blade model that has been chosen. Both men wear informal hats—the man at left, a floppy cavalier hat; the one at right, a comfortable-looking lord's hat with a rolled-up edge.

11

from Apparel Arts, Spring 1936, vol. vi, no. iia

Uncommon Stylishness for the Common Man

Understated, conservative clothes need not be dowdy. The herringbone fabric of the suit shown here is a classic sturdy worsted that has been styled into a long-roll double-breasted model, which at one time could have been considered unusual but is now acknowledged as an elegant variation of a traditional style. The serious effect made by the black tie is lightened by the choice of a white pearl stickpin and an oxblood-striped madras shirt. The elegance of the outfit is reinforced by the addition of a plain breast-pocket handkerchief, while the wide-spread collar adds interest. To complete the look, a gray or blue overcoat and a black homburg would be just right.

from Apparel Arts, Winter 1935, vol. vi, no. ia

The Art of
Self-Salesmanship

Regardless of what his business is, every man has something important to sell. That is himself. And one of the first steps in self-salesmanship is the device of putting yourself on the inside of a persuasive outfit such as this. The smart but not smart-aleck suit is the single-breasted three-button model with peak lapels shown here. The lapel rolls to the top button and the suit is fastened at the middle button; the pockets are without flaps. With this suit is worn a deep tan shirt with a wide-spread collar to match. The tie is black with white polka dots, and the black shoes are in the blucher model. Incidentally, the combination of black and brown is currently considered very smart.

from Apparel Arts, Fall 1936, vol. vi, no. iia

The University Man

Whatever experimentation may be taking place on this page is confined to new brands of tobacco, for the articles of apparel are either staples or pretty well-established fashions. One of the best-selling models in America, among discriminating men, is the two-button notched-lapel single-breasted brown cheviot coat with a diagonal self-pattern worn by the student at the left. The lovat-colored wool cheviot coat with a blue overplaid was originally introduced by the Duke of Windsor when he was the Prince of Wales; it is single-breasted and has peak lapels, raglan shoulders, fly front, slash pockets, and cuffed sleeves. The balance of the outfit consists of a white oxford button-down-collar-attached shirt, a wool tie with spaced figures, a green-and-white houndstooth-check wool muffler, a brown snap-brim hat with a black band, green six-by-three ribbed wool hose, and brown reversed calf shoes. The other student wears a three-button notched lapel cheviot suit with fashionable colored stripes, a two-tone herringbone cashmere pullover, a cotton flannel shirt with a colored overcheck, a solid-colored tie, a green Tyrolean hat, wing-tip brogues, and reversible tweed and gabardine coat.

*The Collegiate Theme
of Brown and Gray*

Ever since the Oxford and Cambridge fashion influence was first felt in the 1930s, the combination of an odd brown jacket with gray flannel pants has been a favorite of the college man. Variations on the theme are acceptable, however. Here the undergraduate is wearing a three-button notched-lapel Shetland jacket with a dark overplaid and side vents—an important fashion note—and patch pockets with flaps. The ensemble is completed by a blue-and-white-striped oxford shirt with attached collar, a striped crochet tie, a blue cashmere sleeveless sweater, a brown felt snap-brim hat, and brown suede shoes; the shoes shown are bluchers, but buckskin brogues would be just as suitable. This casual combination is as proper for country wear as it is for college dress.

15

from Apparel Arts, *Advance Spring 1935, vol. v, no. iia*

From Palm Beach to the Riviera

Studied nonchalance—in French, *degágé*—is the look that is aspired to in resort wear. The combination of the comfort-stimulating qualities of a warm climate and the deliberately complex social routine found at resorts require that just such a level of casual smartness be attained. In the above ensemble, this is created through the combination of a burgundy polo shirt and a tailored suit of natural tan garbardine, with eight-inch side vents. Brown buckskin shoes (with varnished black leather soles and heels), a lightweight felt porkpie hat, a foulard handkerchief, and a red carnation finish the look. A slightly different effect could be created by wearing the handkerchief around the neck.

from Apparel Arts, September 1938, vol. ix, no. ia

High Temperature Togs

Jamaica is one of the smartest gathering places in January for Englishmen and Americans. Hotter than Bermuda, it calls for the most lightweight summer clothes, and the best advice for that Jamaica-bound cruiser is to take along shorts, for everyone there wears them. The two outfits shown here being worn at the cocktail hour are just about standard attire for the entire day up until evening. The one at the left consists of a native madras shirt in a bold, colorful print, with half sleeves and an open collar; colonial khaki drill shorts in a popular model, with the waistband extended to the side buckle; and red canvas rope-sole shoes. The man entering the bar is wearing gray flannel shorts and a lightweight hemp-color jacket with patch pockets. An interesting innovation on this jacket, which is probably made of Palm Beach cloth or some other lightweight washable fabric, are the nickel buttons. Under the jacket is a lightweight lisle or mesh half-sleeve sport shirt. A dash of color is provided by the Indian print neckertie, and the Jippi Jappa hat with telescoped crown, lightweight wool anklets, and blue canvas shoes with rubber soles are cool and practical accessories.

For Tropical Nights

Below, far left: A single-breasted white-shawl-collar dinner jacket with midnight-blue dress trousers, a pleated shirt with fold collar, black tie, and a maroon cummerbund.

Below, left: A double-breasted shawl-collar silk dinner jacket with black dress trousers, a soft shirt with a ribbon-shape black tie, a native coconut straw hat with a white puggree band, and a green silk pocket handkerchief.

from Apparel Arts, October-November 1938, vol. ix, no. ii

Above: The new boater straw hat with an extremely wide dark-colored band, a patent leather monk-front dress shoe, a patent leather pump, a blue velvet formal house slipper with a gold monogram, worn by well-dressed men at house parties in Palm Beach and other Southern resorts.

Above, right: Evening blue—a new shade for dinner jackets worn in Southern climates and made in a double-breasted model in lightweight tropical fabrics, with a self-faced shawl collar. It's shown here with a silk shirt, a black thistle-shape tie, a boater hat with a wide blue band, patent leather evening pumps, and a camel's hair coat for cool evenings.

II

Suits, Sports Jackets, Odd Trousers, and Topcoats

"Gentlemen's clothes are a symbol of the
power that man must hold and
that passes from race to race."
— *F. SCOTT FITZGERALD*

Up until the late eighteenth century, it was often the man who
dressed more flamboyantly than the woman, his wardrobe filled with
laces and bows as well as high-heeled shoes with shiny buckles.
Even our presidents were not immune, as a sartorially splendid
George Washington appeared at his first Inaugural wearing a
brocade jacket, lace shirt, silver appointments, and high-heeled
shoes with diamond buckles.

However, as the country changed, so did clothing styles.
With the emphasis on democracy and the glorification of the
common man, clothing became less ornate, less ostentatious. By the
time Thomas Jefferson was inaugurated, he followed the fashion of
his time by taking the oath wearing a plain blue coat, drab colored
waistcoat, green velveteen breeches with pearl buttons, yarn stockings, and slippers.

At the turn of this century, menswear was still heavily
influenced by the Victorian era, as reflected in suits which at times
resembled an extension of the upholstered look of the Victorian
furniture popular in American homes in the period.

And yet the first decade of this century saw the important
introduction of the sack suit, a style characterized by any shapeless
coat without a waist seam, the body and skirt having been cut in one
piece, and the Ivy League–style clothing from England. It was also
during this period that certain other fashion innovations began to
appear, such as the polo coat (introduced from England by Brooks

1903

19

1913

1923

Brothers around 1910) and the button-down collar (also introduced by John Brooks, in 1900, after he'd discovered it being worn by polo players in England in order to prevent flapping during play).

The 1920s were a time of experimentation, as the suit silhouette turned to the natural-shoulder look, and the first sports jacket—the Norfolk, modeled after the hunting suit worn by the Duke of Norfolk in the early eighteenth century—was produced. This decade also saw the rise and fall of jazz clothing, which had little semblance of balance or respect for the human form, with its inordinately long, tight-fitting jackets and narrow trousers; the cake-eater suit, named for college students who wore this slightly exaggerated copy of the natural-shoulder suit; and the knicker suit, featuring plus-four knickers that fell four inches below the knee. The 1930s was undoubtedly the most elegant period for menswear, as men gravitated toward the English drape style and the sportswear industry exploded. The British drape suit made it safely into the 1940s, though it was then referred to as the British blade, British lounge, and, finally, as the "lounge suit," a fitting name for its casually elegant style.

World War II resulted in a marked austerity in dress, due in large part to the restrictions placed on the clothing industry by the War Production Board. After the war, men were ready for another change in their clothing styles, and in 1948 the "bold look" began to be seen.

The 1950s are best remembered for the "gray flannel suit" worn by the conservative businessman. Now men were back to the natural-shoulder silhouette. As reported in *Apparel Arts' 75 Years of Fashion*, "No style was ever so firmly resisted, so acrimoniously debated—or more enthusiastically received in various segments of the industry. Natural shoulder styling eventually became the major style influence. Brooks Bros., once a 'citadel of conservatism,' became a font of fashion as the new 'Ivy Cult' sought style direction. Charcoal and olive were the colors."

In addition to the introduction of man-made fibers, this period also saw the arrival of the Continental Look from France and Italy, featuring short jackets and broad shoulders, a shaped waistline, slanting besom pockets, sleeve cuffs, short side vents, and tapered, cuffless trousers. This "slick" look made little inroad on those who were staunch adherents of the more conservative Ivy League look, but it was a significant phenomenon nonetheless, as it moved Americans further away from the stylish elegance of the 1930s.

The sixties brought the Peacock Revolution—a phrase popularized in this country by George Frazier, a former columnist for *Esquire* magazine and the *Boston Globe*—which began on Carnaby Street in London and featured a whole array of new looks, including the Nehru jacket and the Edwardian suit. In contrast to the fifties, during which time choices were limited, a wide range of alternatives was now available as the focus moved to youth and protest. The designer Pierre Cardin even created an American version of the slim-lined European silhouette, which, along with the immense popularity of jeans, led to the acceptance of extreme fittedness in clothing—a far cry from the casual, comfortable elegance of preceding generations.

During this period the American designer Ralph Lauren was attempting to convince the American male that there was a viable alternative to this high-style clothing. This alternative was a version of the two-button shaped suit with natural shoulders that had been introduced by Paul Stuart in 1954 and briefly popularized by John Kennedy during his presidency. Lauren updated the Stuart suit by using the kind of fabrics usually reserved for custom-made suits and dramatizing the silhouette by enlarging the lapel and giving more shape to the jacket. Lauren's following remained small, however, as most men leaned toward the jazzier Cardin-style suit.

The seventies were the era of the designer. They were also a time of intense fashion experimentation, coming at a point when the largest growth in the number of people buying fashions occurred and manufacturers tried desperately to capture the one-third of the buying public that was spending two-thirds of the money. Toward the end of the decade, after years of following the fitted clothing styles of Milan and Paris, there was a dramatic turnaround as a number of European designers and manufacturers began biting off pieces of the American style of dress. Brooks Brothers' baggy garments and button-down shirts, both indigenously American, began to be produced in European versions, for Europeans had suddenly become attracted to the looser, more comfortable style of dress and were eschewing the tight-fitting silhouette they'd embraced in the past.

1933

1943

FRED ASTAIRE—*No one wore clothes as well as Fred Astaire.*
Like the Duke of Windsor, once he adopted a new style, such as the
puff-style fold for handkerchiefs, it immediately entered the repertoire
of classic dressing.

While the European look still retained a foothold among American men (represented by designers such as Giorgio Armani, Basile, and Gianni Versace), the pendulum had begun to swing in the direction of a less stylized, more natural-fitting garment. A new generation of American designers joined Ralph Lauren in presenting an updated, purely American style of clothing.

Today American men's designers are continuing to rediscover the traditions of their past, exploring the American heritage in menswear. Of particular interest to most is the 1930s, the era of elegance, in which designers continue to find much to inspire them. Yet the experience of the last twenty years has taught them that men want not only quality, shape, and elegance but comfort as well. Clothes that lead the marketplace today are made of high-quality materials. They are soft and comfortable, but their designs still reflect the qualities of traditional Old World style.

For nearly two hundred years now, men in prominent positions have been going to work wearing proper business suits. Over the years, there have been occasional rebellions against this custom, and, in fact, a mere twenty years ago the future of business suits in this country looked bleak, as dire predictions of men appearing at work wearing jump suits and the like abounded. Yet today, perhaps more than ever before, the business suit is the accepted uniform of the successful entrepreneur.

Naturally, this brings to mind the following question: Why has the business suit enjoyed this longevity? What purpose does it serve? Why should a man even bother wearing one when it seems to limit self-expression and stifle individuality?

Perhaps a starting point in responding to these questions appears in an advertisement placed by the pre-eminent men's clothing store, Paul Stuart, which states that "a proper function of the business suit is to offer a man a decent privacy so that irrelevant reactions are not called into play to prejudice what should be purely business transactions."

While this is certainly true, there is no reason why a man in a business suit has to look bland. Even in a business situation it is possible to dress within certain professional parameters while still managing to avoid the trap of looking as if one just walked off the assembly line. The business suit can and should at least offer the suggestion of character and a sense of individuality. If, for instance, one works in advertising as opposed to banking, one can get away with a bit more verve in a suit rather than adhering to the more conservative look required in the latter profession. But even a man working in banking should not exempt himself from thinking about dress, for whatever one wears says something about the wearer.

Phototeque

DOUGLAS FAIRBANKS, JR.—*He carried the sartorial gospel of the Duke of Windsor—cutaway-collar shirts, Windsor knots, suede shoes, double-breasted suits—to both Hollywood and New York.*

More than any other single item of clothing, it is the suit that ultimately determines the overall style of a man's dress. Although the shirt, tie, and hose all have an important contribution to make to a man's style, none plays nearly so major a role as the suit, which, since it covers 80 percent of the body, actually defines the general mood and impression of one's appearance. Accessories should relate to the suit and not vice versa. To think otherwise would be tantamount to beginning the decoration of an empty apartment by first purchasing an ashtray.

THE SILHOUETTE

"The silhouette" is the term used by the clothing industry to describe the cut or shape of a suit. Women have long realized that the shape of a garment sets the tone of their appearance, but only recently have men realized that they too have a choice of styles that accomplish the same important ask for them.

For this reason, the silhouette should be the primary consideration in the purchase of any suit. The fabric and details, which may add to a suit's attractiveness, and even the fit should be of secondary concern, since it is the silhouette that actually determines the longevity of the garment. If this statement sounds the least bit dubious, think of the tight-fitting rope-shouldered, wide-lapeled, flared-bottom suits of fifteen years ago. Where are they now? In all likelihood, if one still owns these garments, it's been some time since they've seen the light of day.

Today there are three distinct silhouettes that have demonstrated their longevity: the sack suit, the European-cut suit, and the updated American-style suit. The first two choices offer distinctly different approaches to dressing: the sack disguises the figure of a man, while the European model leaves little to the imagination. The third style, the updated American-style suit, is almost an amalgam of the other two, hiding the body as well as flattering it. To my mind, it is the one silhouette that looks most comfortable on the American physique: casual, but eminently proper, stylish but without the studied elegance of the European model.

The Sack, or Brooks Brothers Natural-Shoulder, Suit

The sack, or the Brooks Brothers natural-shoulder, suit has been, for almost a century now, the backbone of American clothing. First popularized near the turn of the century, it was a silhouette characterized by a shapeless, nondarted jacket with narrow shoulders (which were soft and unpadded) as well as by flap pockets, a single rear vent, and a three- or four-button front. Designed large in order to fit many sizes, it was the first mass-produced suit and it looks it. After all, it was not called the sack suit for nothing.

Perhaps the biggest strength of the sack silhouette is also its basic weakness: it hides the shape of its wearer and takes away any sense of individuality. The reason it has managed to exist successfully for such a long period of time is simply that it appeals to the common denominator. Since it is so anonymous, it offends no one, enabling the wearer to walk into any environment and be acceptably attired.

For those seeking anonymity in their clothing, or wishing to hide an ungainly figure, this may be an acceptable style. But for anyone else, the sack-style suit is woefully inappropriate.

The sack suit.

The European Silhouette

Only since the late 1960s has the European-cut silhouette been a major factor on the American scene. This shape relies upon severity of line to project its style. The dominant shape and style in France and Italy for the past thirty years, it has been maintained in a jacket with squarish shoulders, high armholes, and a tight fit through the chest and hips. It is two-buttoned, its back is usually non-vented, and it has a much more structured feel to it than the sack suit. The trousers tend to have a lower rise and fit more snugly through the buttocks and thigh, sitting just under the waist so that one feels them fitting through the hips and thigh, hugging the line of the leg.

As Stephen Birmingham pointed out in *Vogue*, European men liked to " 'feel' the clothes they wore . . . a man in a European-cut suit was very much aware that he was inside something. Sitting down was a delicate operation, and crossing the legs was not to be undertaken lightly. . . . "

In the 1960s and '70s, the European fit gained much popularity in this country, in part because of the mass acceptance of jeans and the notion that clothes ought to express a man's physicality. This silhouette offered a radical alternative to the sack suit and appealed particularly to women, who perhaps unintentionally promoted this exaggerated style, which emphasizes a man's sexuality at the cost of subtlety and comfort. While it is true that a man wearing this silhouette did look thinner, it is also clear that he was compromising taste and style in order to feel thin.

After the initial excitement of this style wore off, American men realized they were projecting a character that was not their own. Europeans, after all, have long dressed in a more formal, studied manner. Their clothing evolved to reflect not only their thin and lithe body types but also their penchant for elegance and formality. Americans, on the other hand, have always preferred a more subtle and casual style. With their broader shoulders and wider chests, they require a softening in the lines of their clothing, not the hard angles identified with the European styles. Recognizing this, they are returning in greater numbers to endemic styles that are designed to complement their larger physiques; clothing that is soft and comfortable, but with a tasteful subtlety that is the purest idiom of the American heritage.

The European-styled suit.

The Updated American Silhouette

The updated American silhouette is a combination of the best elements of the sack and the European-cut suit. The jacket has some of the same softness and fullness through the chest and shoulder areas as the sack, to which it adds some of the European notion of shape.

Long the staple of fine dressers, from Clark Gable to Fred Astaire to Cary Grant, this soft, shaped suit was essentially a spin-off from the sack. The three-button sack coat was modified to a two-button version with some suppression at the waist by Paul Stuart. As mentioned earlier, this style was then modified further by Ralph Lauren, beginning in the mid-1960s. Both his espousal of it and the subsequent support of a score of young American designers gained for this updated American style the national recognition and the widespread acceptance it has today.

Like the European model, the new American-style jacket is tapered at the waist, giving the wearer something of a V-shaped appearance. The jacket, with its two-button design, has a longer lapel roll. In further contrast to the sack, this style also has a somewhat higher armhole and the chest is a bit smaller. All these details work to give it more definition than its dour predecessor.

These modifications give the updated American suit a freedom that allows the materials to adapt themselves to the wearer's physique. This is as it should be. Angular clothing tends to impose itself on the body. It has its own shape, and the wearer must fit into it rather than the other way around. The adaptation of clothing to the wearer's physique, on the other hand, is the ideal expression of oneself. Like a good haircut, the cut of a suit should never call attention to itself. Elegance or style can be achieved only through softness of line. This is why the updated American-style suit jacket has a modified natural shoulder and is cut with a slight taper at the waist, while the trousers take their line from the shape of a man's leg.

The updated American suit.

THE DETAILS

Lapels

Lapels have always been a reflection of the fashion of the moment, widening or shrinking in size to suit the taste of stores or individual designers. This is unfortunate, since their size should never be a matter of whim but always a reflection of the jacket's proportions.

The lapel of a well-styled suit should extend to just a fraction less than the halfway mark between collar and shoulder line. In general, this size means a width of approximately 3½ inches, thus honoring the main principle of classic tailoring, which is that no part, no detail, should violate the integrity of the whole.

Pockets

The flaps on the pockets should be consistent with the size of the lapels—neither too large nor too small. Like the lapels, they should not draw particular attention to themselves. In addition, their actual size should conform to that of the jacket. Patch pockets are fine on sports jackets or sporty suits, but for a dressy suit, a flap pocket or jetted pocket is more appropriate. The jetted pocket is the most dressy, which is why it is traditionally found on the tuxedo. The flap pocket will put a touch more thickness on the hip, while the slit pocket gives a slimmer look.

A skimpy lapel.

An oversized lapel.

The lapel should extend slightly less than
halfway across the chest of the jacket.

Vents

Jacket vents have a military heritage. Before the advent of the automobile, soldiers traveled by horse and thus clothes were adapted accordingly. The slit in the tails of the coat permitted it to fall on each side of the horse, allowing greater comfort and freedom of motion for the wearer. This comfort and ease carried over into walking and sitting, as vents allow trouser pockets to be more accessible and sitting more comfortable.

There are three types of jacket vents: the non-vented jacket,

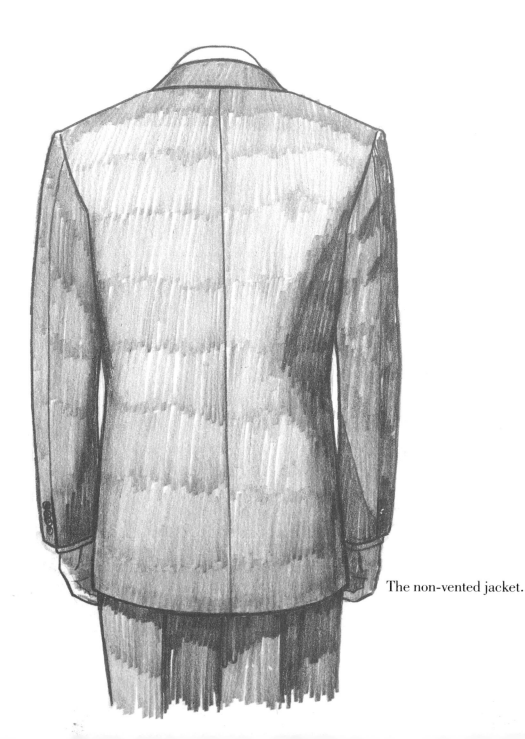

The non-vented jacket.

favored by Europeans; the double-vented jacket, favored mostly by the English; and the single-vented jacket, favored by Americans.

The ventless jacket has wonderful form but functions poorly as a design. Whenever you choose to put your hands in your pockets, or sit down, there is no place for the jacket to go, and so it creases and bunches up in the back.

The center-vented jacket.

The single-vented jacket gives the wearer a boxy look in back by cutting him precisely in half, and when one puts one's hands in the pockets, the jacket appears to split open down the middle, often exposing the belt, the shirt, and the buttocks.

Those who were the best-dressed in the 1930s wore either the double-vented or the non-vented jacket.

Side vents extend the line of the trousers past the jacket hem, giving a man an added sense of height.

However, the double-vented jacket gives added shape to the garment by emphasizing the outside lines of the body. When the wearer is walking, you can see movement on the side, as the jacket corresponds to the movement of the leg. This fluidity helps create a more attractive silhouette. Moreover, the distance from the floor to the bottom of the jacket is lengthened by an observer's eye moving smoothly up the length of the vent, thus giving the wearer the illusion of greater height. Beyond aesthetics, the double-vented jacket is a perfect example of form and function uniting. This is evident when you sit down or put your hands in your pockets: the flap comes up, which allows the jacket to avoid creasing and the buttocks to remain covered.

The only time one might avoid the double-vented jacket is if a man is excessively wide hipped and broad in the rear. Here, the single-vented jacket can do more to camouflage breadth.

The height of the vents should correspond to the bottom of the flap on one's jacket pocket. This means a slit of between seven to nine inches on a size 40 regular. If higher, the vents will simply call attention to themselves.

The side-vented jacket.

FIT

Once you've selected the proper silhouette, the next move is into the fitting room. Years ago, when men's fashions were less fickle and tailors were better versed in the manners of correct dress, this was a reasonable act of faith. Unfortunately, this is not the case today. In all but the very finest stores, today's tailor is simply another cog in the assembly line. He is anxious to get you out with as few alterations and as little cost to the store as possible.

Frankly, then, it is not a good idea to put yourself completely in the hands of the store's tailor, who, more likely than not, has no particular point of view regarding fit. At best, he might offer a strange hybrid of his training, what the store has to offer, and the moment's fashion. As a rule, a customer doesn't know exactly what he wants, and unless the store sells only one style of clothing, he will find himself totally at the mercy of its tailor.

To combat this, it's a good idea to know at least some of the basic principles of fit.

Only one man in a hundred is likely to step into a ready-made suit and find it fits him correctly. Manufacturer standards vary from one to another, so that a size 40 doesn't necessarily mean that the shoulder widths are the same in any two suits. Additionally, no two men are likely to resemble each other in the same way that body parts often don't resemble one another. Both our arms are not exactly the same length, and the curve of the back is often different from one person to the next. This, taken along with the fact that cloths will stretch in varying degrees, means that one must allow for lots of variations in different suits.

There are three critical areas to consider when selecting a suit: the shoulder and chest, the armhole, and the coat length. If the suit selected is not proportioned to your physique in the first place, no amount of tailoring can make it right.

Most men mistakenly use the shoulder width as a gauge for sizing their jacket. The widest part of the body, however, is the distance across the chest and upper arm. It is here that one should look when making a selection. In an effort to make a man appear thinner, many manufacturers cut the shoulder width so narrow that the upper arm protrudes. Make certain, then, that a jacket's shoulders are wide enough to allow the line down the arm from the top edge of the shoulder to fall perpendicular to the ground without bulges. The jacket must be broad enough across the chest to feel comfortable when buttoned. A good test for minimum fullness is to sit down with the jacket buttoned (years ago, it was considered improper to unbutton a jacket in public). If it is not comfortable, then the jacket is not full enough. Return it to the rack and try another. This is very important, since the chest area is critical to the fit of a jacket and, in all too many cases, jackets are cut too small.

Next, consider the armhole, another area that cannot be corrected in the fitting room. It should be cut so that the lower part fits comfortably up into the armpit but is not actually felt. This gives a cleaner look and permits arm movement without the jacket being pulled out of place. Conversely, a low armscye (the technical term for the lower part of the armhole) causes the sleeves to bind when they are raised.

Finally, there is the length of the jacket to consider. You should not attempt to shorten or lengthen a suit jacket any more than an inch or two, or the pocket height will be thrown out of balance, making it either too low or too high. Also, the jacket is usually half an inch longer in the front than in the back. This gives the jacket a line that makes it seem as if the jacket is dropping down into the body rather than standing back away from it.

A narrowly cut shoulder causes the upper sleeve to pull across the bicep.

The jacket shoulders should be wide enough to allow the sleeve to hang perpendicular to the ground.

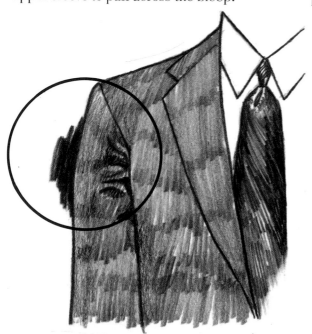

The basic criterion is that the jacket must be long enough to cover the curvature of the buttocks. In general, the jacket ought not be longer than it has to be to accomplish this, since the shorter the jacket, the longer the line of the leg. This is true with the exception of the short man, where having the jacket just cover the buttocks tends to cut him in half (the jacket should be a little longer in this case), and for a very tall man as well, where it causes him to look slightly unbalanced (this also calls for the jacket to be slightly longer).

A shorter jacket gives a longer line to the legs.

A long jacket shortens the line of the leg.

When the length of the jacket is being measured, don't allow your tailor to talk you into the traditional method of dropping your arms and then measuring at the halfway point of the hand. There is simply too much variation in the length of men's arms as well as their bodies to use this as the sole method.

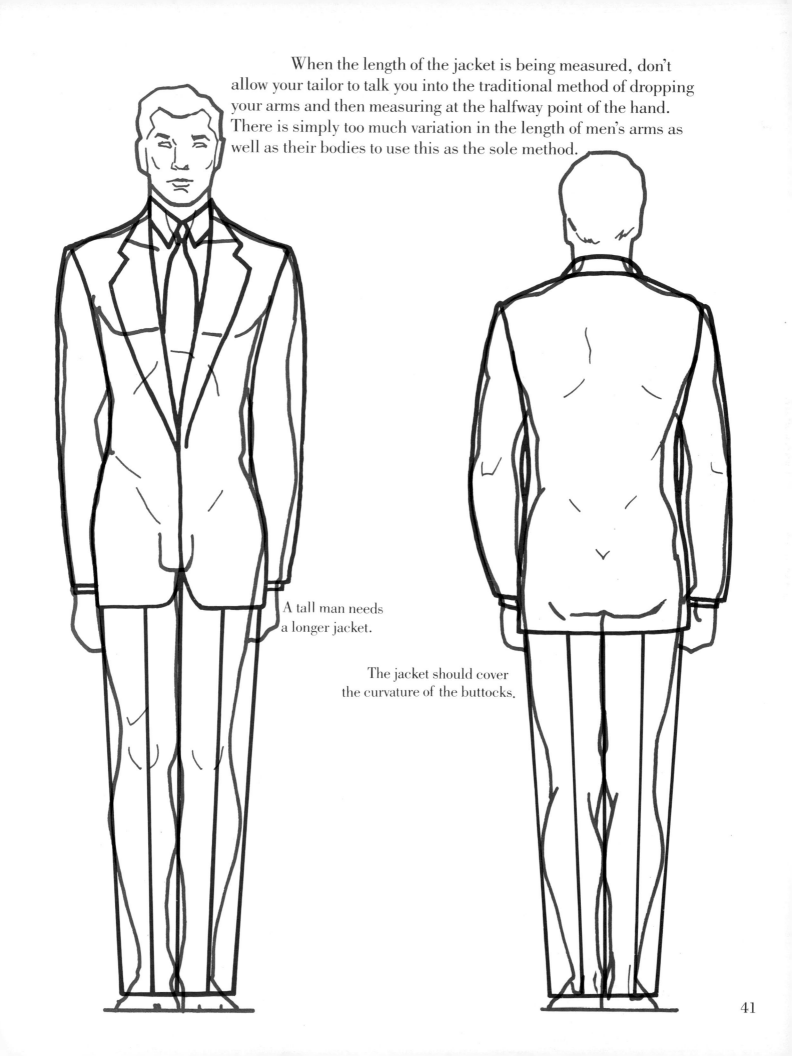

A tall man needs a longer jacket.

The jacket should cover the curvature of the buttocks.

Once the correctly proportioned suit is selected, the fitting room awaits. Bring along those items—wallet, cigarettes, pen, address book, change, and so on—that you would normally carry. It makes no sense to have a breast-pocket billfold produce a bulge when the suit can be altered to hide it. It is also a good idea to wear the haberdashery that would normally accompany this kind of clothing. Wearing a dress shirt with the correct sleeve length and cuff will enable you to better judge the length of the jacket sleeve if it is to show the standard one-half inch of shirt cuff. The height of the dress-shirt collar also helps determine whether the jacket collar is low enough to permit the correct one-half inch of shirt collar to appear above it. A knotted tie controls the position of the shirt-collar points, which should not be covered by the neckline of the vest. Shoes aid in establishing the correct trouser length.

After slipping on the trousers and jacket, with the appropriate items in the pockets and wearing the proper dress shirt, assume a standing position that is comfortable and natural. Fitting a jacket to a stance other than the one normally assumed will ultimately result in the distortion of the line of the jacket when a man stands at ease.

The fitting should begin at the top. The collar should curve smoothly around the back of the neck while the lapels lie flat on the chest. If the jacket collar stands away from the neck, either the manufacturer was careless in attaching it or the collar needs to be altered to fit your particular physique. Since many fabrics fit and drape differently, this is a common alteration that can be handled by

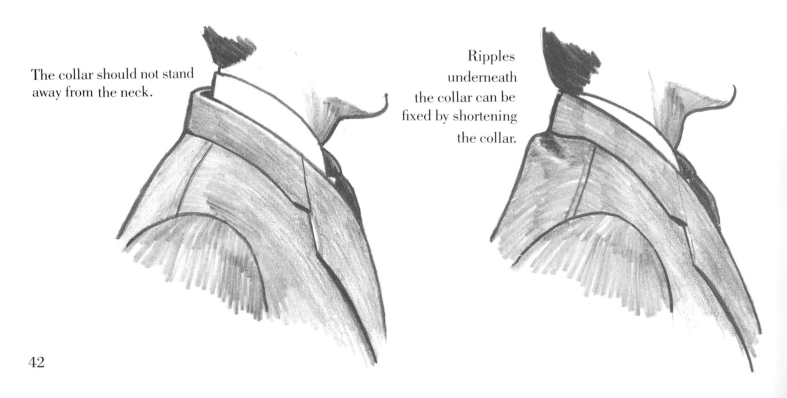

The collar should not stand away from the neck.

Ripples underneath the collar can be fixed by shortening the collar.

most competent tailors. But if you do authorize the store's tailor to make the attempt, be certain you try the suit on in the store after the alterations have been completed. If the collar is still not smooth around the neck, refuse to accept the suit. There is nothing that can destroy the clean lines of a well-tailored jacket more than a collar bouncing on the neck. Instead of allowing the jacket to become a natural extension of the body, the bunching collar makes clear its incompatibility.

Once the shoulders, chest, and neck are satisfactory, continue the inspection downward. The jacket's waist should be slightly tapered, responding to the natural thinning of the body. Be careful not to have it taken in so tightly that the silhouette becomes exaggerated and movements constricted. The jacket is not supposed to fit like a glove (best leave that to the gloves), but it should make reference to the healthy body underneath. Often a great suppression of the waist will make the jacket spread around the hips, opening the vent or vents in the rear. The vents should never be pulled apart so that the seat of the trousers shows. Rather, the vents should fall in a natural line perpendicular to the ground.

Curiously, one of the most important aspects of a suit's alteration is the least complicated: adjusting the sleeve length. Most American men wear their jacket sleeves too long, which makes them appear dowdy. This is probably a vestige of the days when mothers bought coats and jackets with longer sleeves so that their sons would grow into them.

All that business of measuring up from the thumb a prescribed number of inches is a waste of time. Merely let your arms hang down naturally. Then have the sleeves shortened (or lengthened) to the point where the wrist and hand meet. Remember to make sure that the tailor measures both sleeves, since arm lengths differ. The one-half-inch band of "linen" between sleeve and hand is one of the details that go into making a definably well-dressed man.

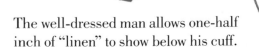

The well-dressed man allows one-half inch of "linen" to show below his cuff.

Vests

The vest as we know it today originated with the postboy waistcoat of nineteenth-century England. It was worn for warmth by the postboy, or postillion, who rode as guide on the horse attached closest to the coach.

Up until World War II, men always wore vests in the wintertime with their single-breasted suits. In recent years the vagaries of fashion have brought this custom in and out of favor. "Fashion" should not be your guide. If you have an opportunity to purchase a vest with your suit, do so. There are numerous advantages to owning a vest, not the least of which is the increased versatility of a three-piece suit. A suit worn with a vest always gives a slightly dressier look.

Vests should fit cleanly around the body, covering the waistband of the trousers and peeking just above the waist button (or middle button) of the suit jacket. Good vests are often cut so that one doesn't button the bottom button, a tradition that began when a member of English royalty appeared at a public function with his bottom button mistakenly undone. This faux pas was picked up by the middle class and has remained with us ever since, producing a casual, somewhat more open look.

Of course, there's no sense wearing a vest if it's not worn correctly. When the jacket is buttoned at the waist, one should be able to see just a small part of the vest above it. Any higher than this and the effect becomes strained, concealing too much of the tie as well. Also, the neckline of the vest should not cover the collar points of the dress shirt but should instead clip them slightly. In addition, the entire elegance of a three-piece suit is destroyed if the trousers are worn on the hips, below the inverted **V** at the bottom of the vest. This allows the shirt or belt to interrupt the smooth transition line from vest to trousers.

A well-made vest has a definite waistline, which is where the waistline of the trousers should hit. The front of the proper vest is normally made from the same fabric as the suit, while the back uses the same fabric as the sleeve lining of the suit jacket.

Vests are adjustable in the rear and traditionally have four slightly slanted welt pockets—two just below the waist and two breast pockets. The breast pockets are deep enough to hold a pair of glasses or a pen, while the shallow lower pockets afford one the option of sporting a pocket watch.

The vest should just peak above the waist button of the suit but not so high that it covers up too much of the tie.

Trousers must be worn on the waist when one is wearing a vest. Otherwise, the shirt and waistband show.

45

Trousers

In the last twenty years, the popularity of jeans and European-style pants has unfortunately accustomed most young men to wearing trousers that are too tight and rest on their hips. Trousers were originally made to be worn with suspenders, which held them on the waist, not the hips, and that is where they look and hang best. No well-dressed man would wear trousers that rested anywhere else. This is not an arbitrary gesture. Every man, no matter how thin, has a slight bulge in his stomach area. When trousers are worn on the waist, they pass smoothly over this bulge in an even drape. Furthermore, waist-worn trousers emphasize the smallness of the waist. They sit there comfortably, supported by the hips. Trousers worn on the hip, however, must be belted tightly, for there is nothing to hold them up. In consort with a vested suit, trousers resting on the hip can only detract from the overall appearance, particularly when there is a gap between vest and trouser top. There is nothing more unsightly—and nothing that draws more attention to the waist—than to have a visible bunching of the shirt or the belt sticking out from between the vest and trousers. The solution is to reaccustom yourself to the way men used to wear trousers. It made sense then and it still does today.

The line of the trousers should follow the natural contours of the body, tapering slowly from hip to ankle. With a waist of 30 to 34 inches, the trousers should have legs with circumferences of 21 to 22 inches at the knees and 18 to 19½ inches at the bottom. Such a description obviously eliminates all types of bell-, flair-, and straight-bottom trousers. These styles, which run counter to the natural lines of the body, call attention to themselves, often cutting the wearer off at the knees. This is especially damaging to someone of small stature, who ends up looking even shorter.

Traditionally, the width of the bottom of a man's trousers was cut to balance the size of his shoe. This means that the width should generally correspond to three-quarters of the length of a man's shoe. The relationship between shoe and trouser bottom is also a convincing argument against having a trouser line that is anything but a slight natural taper.

Pleated trousers should be worn on the natural waist.

47

The straight leg.

The flared leg.

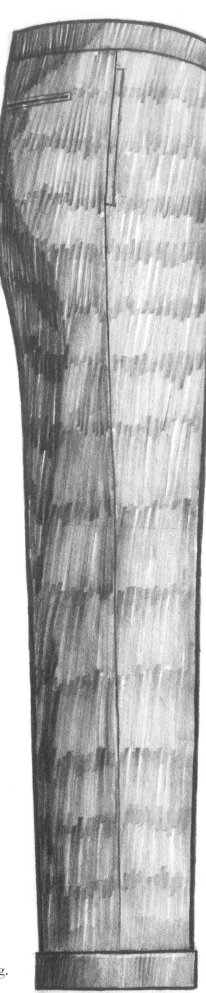

The naturally tapered leg.

When having trousers fitted on the waist, the crotch of the trousers should fit as high as is comfortable. This is especially important for giving a clean fit without sacrificing freedom of movement. The trousers should be worn wide enough across the hips so that there is no pulling across the front pockets. From the side view, the pockets should lie flat on the hips. Trousers to be worn with suspenders should be one-half inch fuller in the waist and must also be a little longer.

Trousers have always been cut in two styles: plain front and pleated front. Traditionally, pleated-front trousers have been the choice of the well-dressed man. Again, there is a functional basis underlying the use of pleats. It was a device created to combine comfort and function. When one sits, the hips naturally widen. The pleat enables the trousers to respond. Additionally, the pleats help to break up the width of the front of the trousers and allow a graceful draping of the cloth, which is particularly evident when a man is walking.

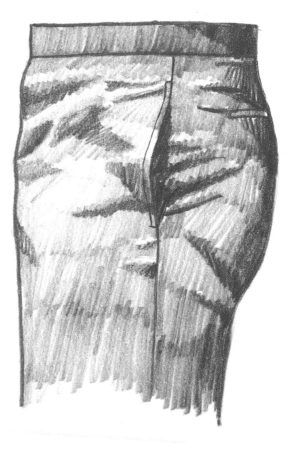

Trousers that fit too tightly pull the pockets open.

The trouser bottom should be approximately three-quarters the length of the shoe.

The width of the trouser leg across the thigh must be large enough so as not to pull open the pleat.

Correct   Incorrect

Pleats will open if trouser is not full enough across the front and thigh.

In fitting pleated trousers, the key is to have enough fullness in the thigh that the pleat does not pull open when one is standing. If one is not prepared to wear trousers with a wider thigh, one is better advised to stick to the plain-front style.

When Abe Lincoln was asked how long a man's legs should be, he replied glibly, "Long enough to reach the ground." Such advice, somewhat modified, might be used to answer the question regarding the proper length of a man's trousers. Trousers should be long enough so that when you walk, your hose does not show.

Cuffed trousers are hemmed on a straight line and should be long enough to break slightly over the instep. Cuffless trousers are hemmed on a slant so that the back falls slightly lower (just at the point where the heel and sole meet).

The use of cuffs is optional, although they do give more weight and pull, thereby emphasizing the line of the trousers. Like any other detail of the suit, cuffs should never be so exaggerated that they call attention to themselves. For this reason, the cuff should be 1⅝ inches if the man is five feet ten inches or less and 1¾ inches if he is taller.

If the trouser is long enough, it should rest on the top of the shoe, producing a slight break.

The double-breasted jacket can be
buttoned on the waist button or
bottom button.

The Double-Breasted Suit

A major style of dress prior to World War II was the double-breasted jacket. Indeed, in the 1930s, 50 percent of all dinner jackets purchased were double-breasted. In fact, it was the Duke of Kent, the Duke of Windsor's brother, who was the first to appear wearing a double-breasted jacket with the bottom button buttoned and with a long, rolled lapel. It wasn't long before other style setters, including Fred Astaire, Douglas Fairbanks, Jr., and others, followed suit. As a result, this became the dominant style of dress right up until World War II, when ready-made fashions took over the marketplace and, because they were less expensive and easier to produce, single-breasted jackets became far more prevalent.

Although the choice between a single- and double-breasted jacket is simply a matter of personal taste, there is no well-dressed man who doesn't have several double-breasted jackets in his wardrobe. This coat is undeniably dressier and, as in the case of pleated trousers, gives a slightly more sophisticated look to the wearer.

The long lapel gives the wearer a sense of added height and stylish elegance.

If one elects to wear a double-breasted jacket, one must keep the jacket buttoned, though there is a choice between buttoning the bottom button or the middle button (but never both). Buttoning only the bottom button gives the wearer a longer line and especially favors the shorter man. Contrary to popular misconceptions, almost anyone except someone exceptionally broad in the hips can wear a double-breasted jacket and look well if the jacket is cut properly. In the 1930s, some of the most elegantly attired Brazilian diplomats, none of whom was taller than five feet six inches, wore double-breasted clothing and it did nothing to mar their appearance. In fact, one of the advantages of double-breasted clothing, especially for the shorter man, is that the uninterrupted line of the lapel when buttoned on the lower button can make a man look somewhat taller, as it cuts diagonally across the body. On the other hand, buttoning the middle or waist button can break up the length of a tall man, thereby balancing him somewhat better.

With the exception of shawl-collared evening jackets, double-breasted jackets should always have peaked lapels. The notched lapels of recent vogue are an abomination and a boon only to manufacturers who produce them less expensively. Traditionally each lapel took a buttonhole. (In Europe they have dropped the right buttonhole.) Historically the wearer took advantage of this arrangement to close up his jacket. Today they are merely an aesthetic necessity, since without them the jacket appears unbalanced. For much the same reason, the double-breasted jacket should be double-vented, though a non-vented jacket is also proper.

There should be no visible space where the collar meets the lapel in a finely designed peaked-lapel jacket.

Sports Jackets

In the first decade of this century, the sports jacket began life simply as the jacket of a dark blue serge suit worn with white flannel trousers and by certain "swells" at fashionable summer resorts.

It wasn't until 1918, however, that the first American sports jacket, based on the Norfolk suit of Harris or Donegal tweed, gained widespread popularity among the wealthy, who could afford a special jacket especially for sport. By 1923 nearly all the best-dressed men at fashionable resorts such as Palm Beach had taken to wearing sports jackets, which were no longer simply suit jackets thrown together with odd trousers. The following year, the blazer jacket was all the rage. This sports jacket was based upon that worn aboard a British sailing vessel of the 1860s, H.M.S. *Blazer*. It seems that the captain of that vessel was disturbed by the way his crew dressed and comported themselves, and so he ordered them to wear dark blue serge jackets on which were sewn the Royal Navy buttons. Thus, they were uniformly dressed, so that their appearance —and one would assume their behavior as well—was markedly improved.

As the years passed and men dressed more informally, the popularity of the sports jacket grew enormously to the extent that today it is a staple of every man's wardrobe.

The fit and styling of a well-cut sports jacket closely follows that of the classic suit jacket. Where the two might differ is in their materials and perhaps in some of the specific detailing. Sports jackets have more visible details, such as swelled or lapped edges on the lapels, patch pockets, leather buttons, or a yoke or belt in the back. These variations are as much a reflection of the independent origins of the two kinds of jackets as it is of their present differing roles.

In fitting a sports jacket, most of the same rules used in selecting a suit apply. However, a sports jacket ought to fit somewhat more loosely in order to accommodate a wool sweater or odd vest.

Today, sports jackets are ubiquitous and worn in a wide variety of situations, though not always appropriately. Do not forget that the sports jacket, because of its origins and tradition, conveys a casual image. While it may seem to be the perfect attire for a weekend or social get-together, it never looks serious enough in a business environment. If in doubt about the formality of a particular occasion, the safer choice is always a suit, since one cannot be faulted for being overdressed, although the reverse is not always true.

Topcoats and Overcoats

Generally speaking, a topcoat is somewhat lighter than an overcoat, but today the line between the two has become blurred, so that the terms are often used interchangeably.

At the turn of the century, due to the oversized suits, overcoats were quite long, ranging anywhere from 42 to 52 inches and extending well below the knee. As time passed, though, overcoats became trimmer and less bulky, with popular styles ranging from the Chesterfield, named for the nineteenth-century Earl of Chesterfield, to the Ulster, which was originally worn in Ireland.

The basic principles of silhouette and fit that guide one in choosing a classic suit should also be followed when selecting a topcoat. As with the suit jacket, the shape of the collar around the neck is the key area of fit. The collar should lie flat and curve smoothly around the neck, not ride up.

When you try on a topcoat, make sure you are wearing a jacket underneath. There should always be enough room for a jacket or sweater (with no feeling that you are being bound), since in most cases that is what you will be wearing underneath. Sleeves should be fitted slightly longer than the jacket sleeve, one-half inch below the wrist. No shirt linen or jacket sleeve should be visible.

Where most men err in fitting their topcoats is in the length. The bottom of the coat should fall just below the knees, or if you prefer a longer topcoat, then six or eight inches below the knees. This length is crucial. When topcoats are above the knee, a man looks bulky and stunted. Because the upper part of the body is massive compared with the rest, and because this massiveness is accentuated even further by the wearing of a jacket covered by a topcoat, the length of the coat is needed to rebalance the body's proportions.

On a purely pragmatic level, long coats offer greater warmth and protection. Why expose the knees and legs to the ice and cold when they can be comfortably enveloped in wool?

On the other hand, one's topcoat should never be so long that it functions as a street cleaner or touches the ground as one climbs steps.

The polo coat in camel hair with a
traditional two-piece belt in back.

57

In the same practical vein, one must wonder about manufacturers who produce topcoats with high rear vents. Not only does one look ridiculous when the wind blows open the long flaps, exposing the seat of one's pants, but it can be awfully cold and uncomfortable. Rear vents should never extend above the bottom curvature of the buttocks.

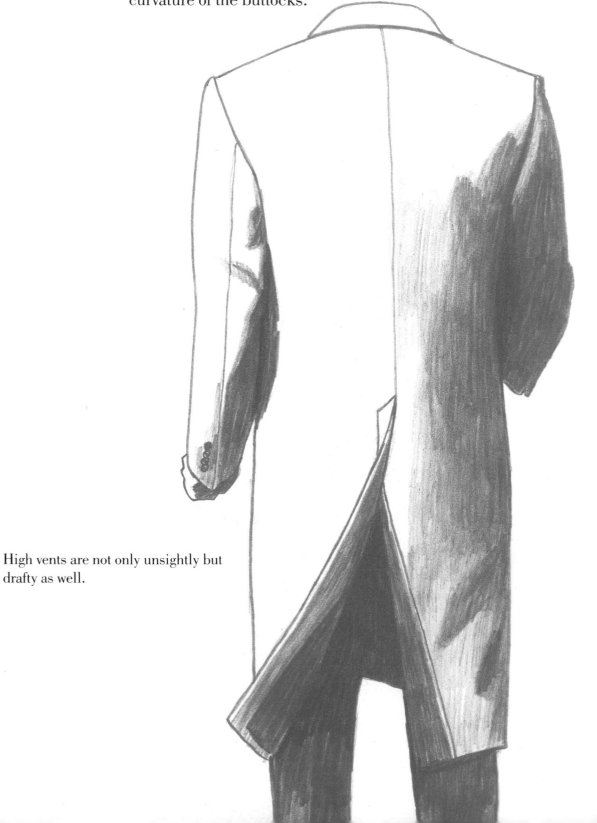

High vents are not only unsightly but drafty as well.

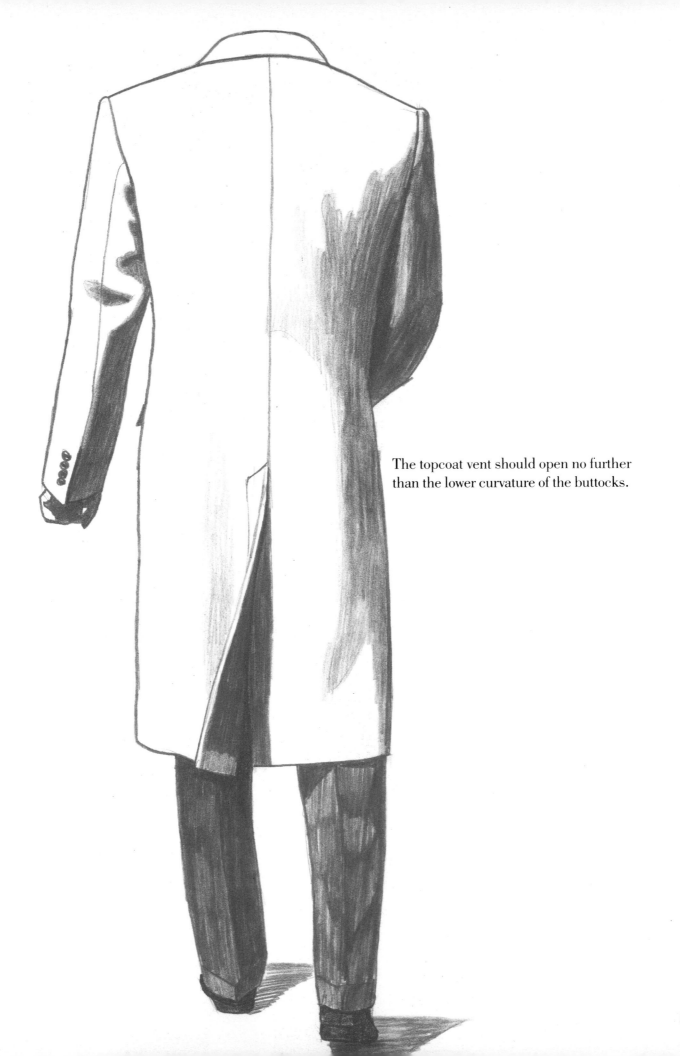

The topcoat vent should open no further than the lower curvature of the buttocks.

A coat worn above the knee looks boxy because it frames the upper mass of the body.

The British warmer.

The Chesterfield coat.

There is a plethora of overcoats manufactured today in a wide variety of styles, but only a few can be considered "classic." These few are certain to retain their stylishness in the future. For daytime wear, this might mean a single-breasted Chesterfield in navy blue or charcoal gray with or without a velvet collar; a single- or double-breasted navy or gray herringbone overcoat; an English fly-front tan covert coat, again, with or without a matching velvet collar; a fawn-colored double-breasted British warmer; or a camel's hair "polo" coat, double-breasted, with a belt in the back. In the evening, consider a Chesterfield overcoat of black wool with a black velvet collar, or a dark tweed with a fur collar.

As I enumerated above, many of these fine coats come in both single- and double-breasted styles. One ought to remember that double-breasted coats tend to be warmer because of the second layer of material that crosses the front of the coat. There are also some handsome coats with raglan-shouldered sleeves. However, unless the raglan shoulders are cut wide enough, the suit jacket will produce a bulge underneath, impairing a smooth drape.

THE DISTINGUISHING QUALITIES OF A WELL-MADE SUIT

Often what distinguishes a fine, well-made suit from all others is simply a matter of the details. In most cases, the presence or absence of these details is a good indicator of the quality or the level of style of the suit in question.

Generally speaking, the more handwork that goes into a suit, the more expensive it will be. For instance, most of the less expensive suits today (those costing under $300) have canvas fused or glued to the front of the jacket in order to stabilize the shape and cloth. In the finer suits, however, the canvas is stitched by hand, so that the cloth tends to shape itself to the body. (The one exception to this is with cotton suits, for which, because they wrinkle, fused fronts may be preferable.)

In most cases, the softer the feel of the suit, the better it is. One might try putting one's hand on the chest and squeezing the cloth. If it is soft to the touch, chances are it's not only a fine fabric but of quality manufacture. Perhaps the easiest way to experience the feeling of wearing a hand-made suit is to try on one manufactured by the Chicago clothing firm of Oxxford. While the design is for the older man, it is the finest quality ready-made suit manufactured today.

Handwork

As stated above, the more pieces of a suit that are sewn together by hand, the better the quality and, naturally, the higher the price will be. Industrial technology today allows clothing companies to make a suit almost entirely by machine, but a fine-quality manufacturer will still insist on having some parts made by hand. Two areas are particularly significant, and one should check them before choosing a suit. First, look under the collar. A fine-quality jacket will have the collar attached to the jacket by hand.

The other important detail involves the setting of the sleeves to the jacket body. If they have been felled by hand, one can count on good fit and proper shape. This is the area that receives the most wear and pressure, so a strong binding is also extremely important. The best suits use fine-quality silk thread.

Hand stitching on the edge of the lapel is another detail one might look for. This stitching has no utilitarian value, but it is a nice finishing touch to a lapel and is evidence of a concern for quality on the part of the manufacturer.

Lining

A lovely trapping of fine tailoring is handsome lining. Traditionally, the body lining was color-coordinated with the suit fabric (this is still occasionally available) while striped linings were used in the sleeves. But the color is less important than the quality of the fabric. Make certain it is soft and neatly sewn into the coat.

Curiously, it is actually more expensive to make a suit without a lining than one with a lining. In an unlined jacket, all the inside seams must be perfectly finished. Yet when manufacturers made and tried to market unlined jackets in an effort to make clothing softer and cooler, American men refused to buy them. They believed that these "unconstructed" jackets must be of lesser quality, or else they simply preferred the ease of sliding into their clothing.

However, a lining does provide a jacket with increased durability as well as helping to maintain its line.

Buttonholes

The buttonholes are another indicator of a suit's quality. Another holdover from the past is the fact that all fine-quality suits have handmade buttonholes. You can tell a handmade buttonhole by looking to see whether it is smooth on the outside and rough on the inside; a handmade one will be just that, but a machine-made one will be smoother and more perfect-looking on both sides. Traditionally, buttons have been sewn on so that they are cross-stitched. The buttonholes should be well-finished, with no threads hanging. If a manufacturer would release a suit with one of its most visible aspects in disrepair, think how little care must have been given to those parts of the suit that don't show.

Real buttonholes on the sleeve—ones that actually function —have long been a symbol of custom tailoring. Mass manufacturers could not employ this detail because stores needed the capability to alter the sleeve length to fit different-size arms. The only way to alter a sleeve that has an open buttonhole is to remove the sleeve from the shoulder and then make the adjustment—a prohibitively expensive alteration. Originally these open buttonholes might have served some real function, such as allowing a man to turn back the sleeves while working or, in the past, for using with detachable-cuff shirts. Today, however, they are simply a symbol.

Whether they are serving a function or not, buttons should be on the sleeves of jackets; four each on suit jackets and overcoats; two or four on sports jackets. The four buttons on a suit should be set closely together, with their edges "kissing," and the edge of the bottom button should be no more than three-quarters of an inch from the bottom of the sleeve.

The one working buttonhole worth having is on the lapel. After all, it is the most visible of all the buttonholes. Besides, a working buttonhole allows the wearer to sport a flower in the lapel, which from time to time can be a wonderful aid to a stylish look. And on those occasions when one must wear a flower, there is nothing considered more outré than the stem being pinned to the lapel. For this reason alone, no fine suit lacks a functioning buttonhole.

Materials

There is only one immutable principle governing the selection of fine suit material: the cloth must be made from natural fibers. This means some type of fine worsted or woolen in the cooler periods of the year—worsted, flannel, gabardine, and so on—and in the summer, if not a tropical wool, then linen, cotton, or silk. There is absolutely no way a man can ever be considered well-dressed wearing a blended suit with more synthetic fibers than natural ones. These fabrics stand away from the body, stiffly retaining their own shape, rather than settling on the individual wearer. No matter how hard one tries, one's suit will somehow always look artificial.

In addition to look and feel, there will be less maintenance required for a natural fiber suit. A fine wool suit rarely has to be dry cleaned. Because air can pass through it, the wool can "breathe" and damp odor from perspiration will readily evaporate. Wool yarn can also return to its original shape. If the trousers are hung from the cuff and the jacket hung on a properly curved hanger after a day's wear, the suit will return to its original uncreased form by the following day.

Perhaps the most important compensation of wearing natural-fiber suits is the comfort one can enjoy having a fabric next to the skin that somewhat simulates its properties. Natural materials have a soft, luxurious feeling. They act like a second skin, letting out perspiration and body heat when necessary and holding in warmth when it's cold outside.

Synthetic fabrics, on the other hand, are forms of plastic. They have no ability to "breathe." In summer, these suits are hot, holding in the warmth of the body; in winter, they offer no protection from the cold. One can choose a suit with 3 to 5 percent nylon reinforcement, but any larger amount of synthetic fiber will begin to undermine the natural material's beneficial properties.

a
t
h
r

The detachable collar remained popular right up until World War I, when returning American servicemen, having lived in their army uniforms for a couple of years, once again discovered the assets of the soft attached collar. Once the boys experienced that kind of comfort around their necks, they weren't about to go back to those stiff, starched collars, and detachable collars soon went the way of the dinosaur.

In the nineteenth century the shirt industry was not particularly sophisticated. As *Apparel Arts* noted in 1931, "A square of cloth gathered into a yoke at the shoulder, with shapeless sleeves and a hole for the neck, was called a shirt. Neckbands had but three sizes: fourteen, fifteen and sixteen inches." But to go that one (or even two) better, shirt sleeves had only a single size: long, to accommodate any length arm. Your shirt didn't fit you so much as you fit your shirt, and if you didn't, well, that was just too bad. In fact, it wasn't until the beginning of the second decade of this century that measured sleeve lengths replaced the arm band as the method of setting one's cuffs correctly, and this, not coincidentally, occurred about the same time that soft cuffs were being introduced on shirts. After a prolonged absence, comfort was finally making a comeback.

Changes came slowly in the shirt industry. It wasn't until the late 1800s, for instance, that color was finally introduced into shirts; and it was about this time that manufacturers found that if they laundered the shirts before offering them for sale, they appealed more to the prospective shopper's eye and, as a result, moved off the shelves that much more quickly.

Innovations continued during the twentieth century. In 1920, the semi-stiff collar was introduced by John Manning Van Heusen; eight years later, Cluett Peabody & Co. invented the Sanforizing process, which prevented the shirt from shrinking when it was laundered; and in the 1950s, Brooks Brothers became the first store to offer a polyester-blend dress shirt, a move that, up until the oil crisis of the late 1970s, kept the cost of shirts down and unfortunately had the effect of sanctioning the use of synthetic fibers in the industry.

Since the 1950s, while manufacturers' changes have been few, styles have changed radically. Paralleling the excesses of the

Peacock Revolution, shirt collars grew to disproportionate lengths while colors took on the nightmarish hues of Day-Glo paints and subway graffiti. Today, the palette has sobered and the collar styles have returned to more traditional proportions that are more in keeping with the current conservative mood of the country.

It's quite simple, really: fine-quality dress shirts are made of 100 percent cotton. Naturally, they cost more than polyester blends, but what you pay for is unrivaled comfort and a look that bespeaks luxury and tradition. As a natural fiber, cotton respects the natural needs of the body. It breathes, allowing the body to cool itself when necessary, and it absorbs moisture when the body perspires. As the article of clothing most in contact with the body, the shirt needs to act almost as a second skin. Cotton performs this function best.

Beyond comfort, finely combed cotton shirtings look better because of the density of their weave as well as because of cotton's ability to take color, thus giving a truer response to dyes. There is a clarity and richness to their color which simply cannot be duplicated with blended fabrics.

The natural sheen of fine cotton shirtings is warm and subtle, not at all like the harshness of pure polyester. Except during the 1920s, when, perhaps due to the influence of those like the fictional Jay Gatsby, there was a brief flirtation with silk, cotton has always been and continues to be the shirting fabric of the well-dressed man.

Once the shirt material has been examined, the next place to look is the shirt collar. Indeed, there are some haberdashers who would suggest that this might be the first place to look, since the collar is all one ever sees of the shirt, that and perhaps one-half inch of cuff. In many respects, the shirt collar plays a role similar to that of the silhouette of the suit. It sets the tone of one's dressing style and is probably the key to the shirt's longevity.

Perhaps the most important aspect to consider is the relation-ship of the shirt collar to one's own physical proportions. Proper balance is the ideal. If a man is large, with a broad face and bullish neck, nothing will appear sillier under his chin than a tiny collar—rounded, spread, or otherwise. Conversely, a high-set collar with 3½-inch points will overwhelm a small man with delicate features.

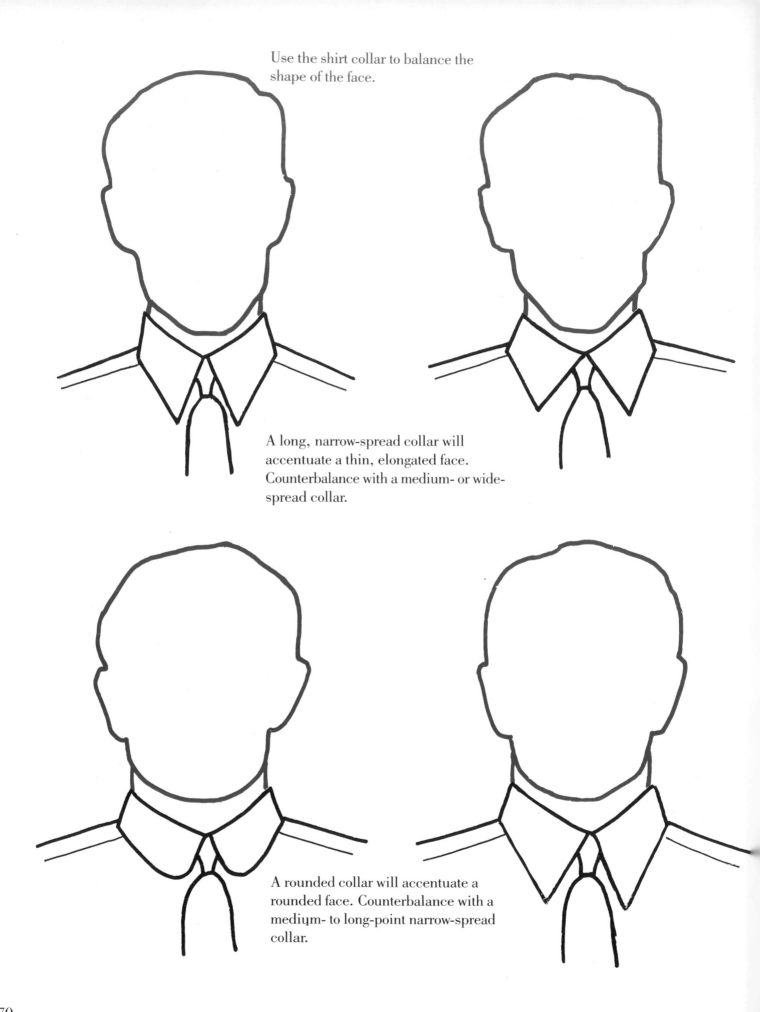

Use the shirt collar to balance the shape of the face.

A long, narrow-spread collar will accentuate a thin, elongated face. Counterbalance with a medium- or wide-spread collar.

A rounded collar will accentuate a rounded face. Counterbalance with a medium- to long-point narrow-spread collar.

70

A man with a long neck requires a higher-banded shirt collar.

A man with a short neck requires a lower-banded shirt collar.

The correct height of a properly fitted shirt collar sits approximately one-half inch above the jacket collar.

For the average-size man wearing a standard regular straight-point collar, the collar points should be no smaller than 2¾ inches nor larger than 3¼ inches. A man much larger would do better with a 3-inch to 3¼-inch collar. Generally speaking, the larger the man, the larger the collar he can take. But one oughtn't push this notion too far. The proportions of the shirt collar can either draw attention to a man's physical irregularities or de-emphasize them, which is generally the more flattering course to follow. Therefore, if you have a short neck, look for shirt collars that lie flat. If your neck is particularly long, a higher band collar seems to shorten its length.

No matter what size your neck is, however, the shirt collar should always show approximately one-half inch of material above the collar of the jacket. In the end, let common sense prevail.

The ideal shirt collar forms an upside down **V**, with the edges of the collar meeting at the throat. No space should be left between the edges. If the shape and width of your tie is appropriate to the shape and size of the shirt collar, no extra space is ever needed. Such collars are not always easy to find today because mass manufacturers want their shirts to fit any size tie and knot. However, one should try to find shirts whose collars have the least tie space between them so that a small elegant knot will not be left in a vacuum between the collar points.

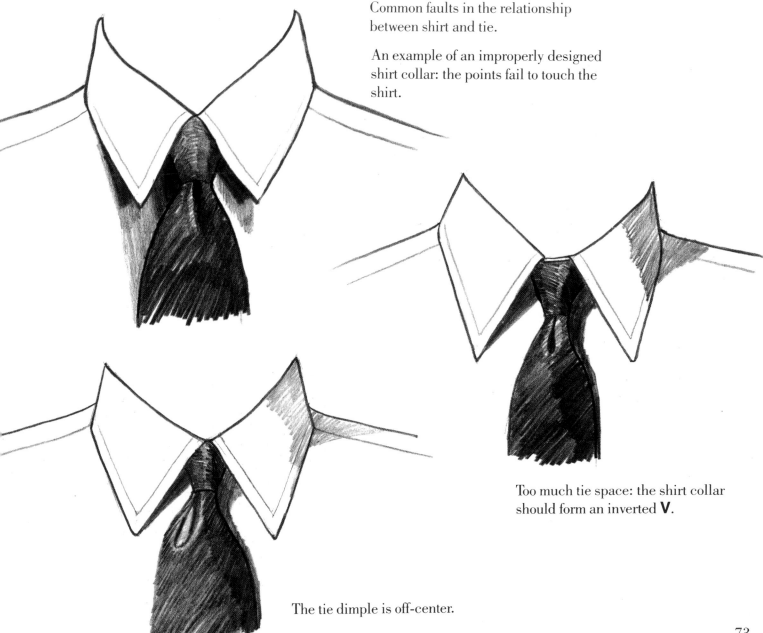

Common faults in the relationship between shirt and tie.

An example of an improperly designed shirt collar: the points fail to touch the shirt.

Too much tie space: the shirt collar should form an inverted **V**.

The tie dimple is off-center.

A Windsor knot is generally too large for a pin collar.

The pin is too long to close the shirt collar around the tie knot.

One more thing to remember about a shirt collar: a fine collar is always stitched around the edges to stiffen and hold the folded material in place. In general, this stitching should not be more than one-quarter inch from the collar's edge. The finer the shirt, the finer the stitching. High-quality shirts are sewn with a single needle, which produces a very small stitch—usually twenty-two to twenty-four to the inch. Contrast stitching will act to destroy the quiet relationship between the tie and shirt and can easily appear to be an affectation. No stitching at all gives the collar a cheap, mass-produced look.

In choosing the proper shirt collar to wear with a specific suit or sports jacket, one must first consider the image the suit projects. Sports jackets and tweedy suits are informal, casual. Obviously, then, they should not be worn with a highly starched white collar but, rather, with a soft button-down or rounded collar, or perhaps even with a straight-pointed collar that can be gathered together with a pin. For dark, more dressy attire, one should wear a stiffer collar with sharp points that are straight or widely spread, such as the short cutaway the Duke of Windsor used to sport. Somehow, a button-down collar just looks too casual after 6 P.M. if one is trying to dress for the evening.

COLLAR STYLES

Today there is a wide spectrum of shirt collars from which to choose. Of these there are seven that a man can add to his wardrobe, confident that they will continue to survive the whims of fashion.

The button-down.

The Button-Down Collar

The button-down collar was first introduced in this country by Brooks Brothers, patterned after the polo shirt worn in England. As explained earlier, the collar was originally fastened down in order to prevent flapping in the player's face during a match. This collar, unlike all others, is soft and meant to remain that way. It is without doubt the most comfortable collar and represents nothing less than the American spirit by producing a casual image so in tune with our heritage. It has been popular every decade since the twenties, and since its origins are definitely in sport, it is not considered a particularly dressy collar. Since it never lies exactly the same way, it offers an unpredictable buckling about the neck, thereby reflecting the wearer's individuality. It is a collar long associated with the Ivy League look and is especially complementary to the natural-shoulder suit. It is appropriately worn with tweed sports jackets and woolen suits. The Brooks Brothers original model remains the best version, for its points are long, permitting a "roll" that changes as the wearer moves. The button-down collar will accommodate a Windsor knot or a four-in-hand, and when worn with a bow tie, it projects the ultimate professorial image.

The straight-point collar.

The Regular Straight-Point Collar

The regular straight-point collar with medium points should be the basic staple of any man's wardrobe. It is a shirt collar that can be worn with any style suit. In the seventies, this collar became very short in length. Today, though it has lengthened somewhat, it is still on the short side, especially in relationship to the width of both the tie and the jacket lapels. Ideally, the collar points should be $2\frac{5}{8}$ to $2\frac{7}{8}$ inches long to balance with the classic jacket lapel width of $3\frac{1}{2}$ inches and the tie width of $3\frac{1}{4}$. Because it embodies the least number of associations, this collar tells the least about the man wearing it. However, its lack of associations allows untold versatility. There is no suit style for which it is inappropriate.

The straight point with pin.

The Pin Collar

This is the same collar as the straight-point except that it is worn with a pin that goes through the collar, with collar bars that snap onto the collars, or with a bar that has a screw and ball that connect through eyelets. Popular during the late twenties, it is a style that is favored by the most meticulous dressers, since it clearly takes more effort to assemble and lock the tie in place. It suggests that the wearer has a highly refined interest and enjoyment in wearing clothes. Shirt collars designed with eyelets for use with a bar are stylish and can be worn with either sports jackets or business suits. Worn with a starched, pointed collar, the shirt is dressy; worn with a softer oxford-cloth collar, the look remains sporty. The first preference should be for the models with eyelets and the screw and ball; the next choice should be the style with the pin through the collar; and finally, the snap-on variety, which has a neat and stylish appearance but does not secure the collar as well as the other two. There is no need to worry about putting pinholes in your shirt collar, as after washing the shirt, the hole will naturally close up. This collar looks best on men with a medium to long neck.

The English cutaway (Windsor).

The Windsor Collar

The Windsor collar was first popularized in the 1930s by the Duke of Windsor in order to accommodate the larger knotted necktie to which he was partial. It is the most formal of all collar styles. Because of its formality, it has never quite made it into the mainstream of American clothing, gaining popularity only during those periods when American dress has been heavily influenced by the English. This is a shame, because with its open angled, starched, stiff collar, it heightens the dramatic gesture of the collar. Though often worn with single-breasted clothing, it looks best with double-breasted jackets since its crisscrossing collar suggests the crossing lines of the jacket. Clearly this style would look highly inappropriate with informal attire such as sports jackets or tweed suits.

The English spread.

The English Spread Collar

Alas, one style innovation not introduced by the Duke of Windsor, the English spread collar is, in fact, attributed to his brother the Duke of Kent, a more conservative but still stylish dresser in his own right. The collar is a dressy one meant to accompany suits or possibly a blazer. The collar itself is less spread than the cutaway Windsor, but because of its high band, it sits farther up on the neck. Its overly large presentation often seems out of balance with today's softer, more naturally styled clothing. The collar has long been a favorite of London's German Street custom shirtmakers and gained international prominence with the marketing success of Turnbull & Asser. Prince Charles as well as his father are two of the most famous adherents to this shirt style.

The tab.

The Tab Collar

The tab collar, yet another style innovation created by the Duke of Windsor, holds the tie in place by utilizing tabs attached to the collar and held together under the knot of the necktie. Though it is actually a more precise way of holding the tie in place than the pin, since the tab is in the same place each time, it is seen as less fussy and thus more acceptable in the business world. Today the tab comes with a snap button or plastic tab. However, the original style, which involves using a brass stud, is still far more elegant.

The rounded (or club).

The Rounded Collar

The rounded, or club, collar, first popularized by English school-boys attending Eton, has been a staple of the Ivy League set since the 1920s. Worn starched with or without a pin, this style complements a dressy suit. Worn soft pinned or unpinned, it looks equally well with a sports jacket. While versatile, the rounded collar does not flatter a man with a round face since it only accentuates the circularity.

Each one of these collar styles has its various adherents and each can look good under the proper circumstances. Thus, unlike the silhouette of a suit, there is no reason a man must confine himself to only one style.

FIT

In fitting a shirt, think first of comfort. The neckband should never choke or chafe, nor should the body of a shirt bind a man's torso. The neckband should fit snugly so that the collar doesn't fall down the neck, with an air space of one-quarter inch in front, allowing the head to turn without chafing the neck. Unfortunately, 80 percent of men wearing dress shirts wear the neckband too tight, either because the shirt has shrunk or because, due to age, the neck has thickened. However, if the neckband is too tight, it will spread the collar, creating a larger space where the tie knot sits. This is not only unsightly, giving a sloppy appearance to the wearer, but is also exceedingly uncomfortable.

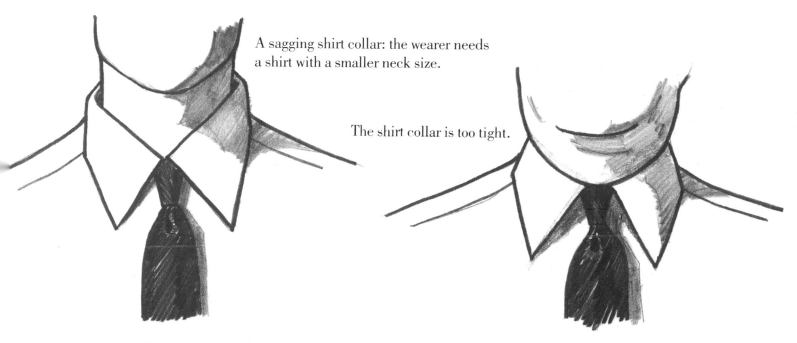

A sagging shirt collar: the wearer needs a shirt with a smaller neck size.

The shirt collar is too tight.

The body of the shirt should have no more material than is necessary for a man to sit comfortably. Excess material bulging around the midriff could destroy the lines of the jacket. If you do buy a shirt with too large a body, a seamstress can take in the side seams or put darts in the back to reduce the size. The darts are actually a bit more practical, since if you put on weight they can be removed. The length of the shirt is also an important concern. It should hang at least six inches below the waist so that it stays tucked in when you move around. It should not be so long, however, that it creates bulges in front of the trousers.

As for the sleeves of the shirt, they should show a full half-inch beyond the sleeves of your jacket. Generally, a good rule to follow is that they should finish approximately one-half inch below the break of the wrist. If you bend your arm and the cuff recedes behind the wrist, the sleeve is too short. A proper size sleeve will allow you to move your arm in any position without withdrawing the cuff. The cuff itself should fit snugly enough to hold its place on the wrist without appearing as a tight bracelet. But it should be small enough that the hand cannot go through it without it being unbuttoned. Or, to put it another way, the cuff should bear some reference to the size of one's wrist.

Cuffs

There are two types of shirt cuffs from which to choose: the barrel and the French. The barrel cuff fastens with one or two buttons. The French cuff is much more expensive to produce, so naturally manufacturers have taken to marketing mainly the barrel cuff. The French cuff, however, is far more elegant. When worn under a dark suit, the double fold of the French cuff combined with the bit of light that is the cufflink adds a richness to a man's attire that a single cuff and button simply cannot replace.

The means by which the cuff itself—either the barrel or French—has been attached to the sleeve is often a reliable indicator of the quality level of the shirt's manufacture. This attachment is no simple task. A big sleeve, one that can fit comfortably around the biceps and forearms, must be reduced in circumference and then sewn to a cuff that fits the smaller wrist. Often the sleeve is simply tapered in its shape so that there is little extra fabric to tuck into the cuff. But if instead the sleeve has been carefully folded into several pleats and then attached to the cuff, the shirt as a whole has undoubtedly been made with care. In England the custom shirtmakers actually sew small pleats in a complete circle around the cuff. French shirtmakers use a symmetrical pattern, folding two or three pleats into the cuff on each side.

A French cuff with sleeve placket and button.

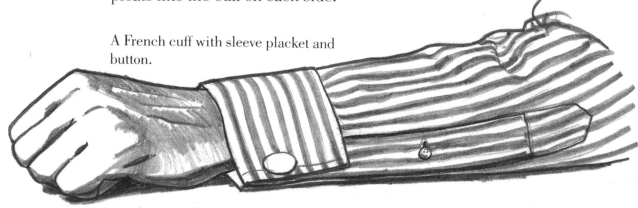

A shirt made with a split yoke.

Plackets, Yokes, and Gauntlets

These three items of obscure terminology can offer further clues to the quality level of a shirt's manufacture.

The placket is that piece of material on the front of the shirt where the buttonholes are placed. In the past, it used to be a separate piece of cloth sewn to the front, but today shirtmakers merely fold the edge of the material to simulate this look. All fine dress shirts are made with a placket that is approximately 1½ inches wide. This placket gives the shirt a definite center line and makes a clean finish where the shirt sides join to be buttoned.

The yoke is the strip of material sewn across the shoulders to attach the front and back pieces of the shirt. Custom shirtmakers use a split yoke—two yokes joined in the center—so that they can adjust each shoulder separately for a custom fit. Occasionally you will still see a split yoke, but unless the shirt has been made especially for you, this detail doesn't serve any real function. However, it does indicate a finer-quality shirt.

"Gauntlet" is the English term for the sleeve placket, that open area just before the cuff. A well-made shirt has a working button on the placket so that this gap can be closed when the shirt is being worn. The gauntlet button originated in order to enable men to roll back their cuffs while washing as well as to hold the cuff in place. Obviously, a gauntlet button is not one of life's dire necessities, though in certain circles a show of bare forearm is considered in as poor taste as a show of skin between hose and trouser cuff. On the other hand, a buttoning gauntlet does permit a better fit around the forearm and is one more indication of a quality shirt.

Mention should also be made here concerning the buttons of a shirt. While most buttons today are of man-made material, a mark of a finer shirt are buttons made of mother-of-pearl. Unfortunately, mother-of-pearl is a more fragile substance than plastic, but its wonderfully deep luster more than compensates for its fragility. A man interested in fine style doesn't mind the effort of having to replace such buttons every once in a while.

Monograms

Monograms are a nice way of personalizing your shirt, though not when they are ostentatiously placed on cuffs or on the collar of a shirt so as to act like a billboard. Keep the lettering simple and the initials discreet (no larger than one-quarter inch high). Place them approximately five or six inches up from the waist, centered on the left half of the shirt. If the shirt has a pocket (and many custom-made shirts do not), center the initials on it.

Shirt monograms are usually associated with custom-made shirts, but they can be sewn on any store-bought model. The extra cost they incur will show people that you care enough about the way you dress to take the time to individualize your shirt, as well as helping to avoid possible confusion when it is sent to be cleaned.

Examples of the proper placement of shirt monograms, with and without pocket.

IV
Neckwear

The history of neckties dates back a mere three hundred years or so, for they came into existence as the direct result of a war. In 1660, in celebration of its hard-fought victory over Turkey, a crack regiment from Croatia (then part of the Austro-Hungarian Empire), visited Paris. There, the soldiers were presented as glorious heroes to Louis XIV, a monarch well known for his eye toward personal adornment. It so happened that the officers of this regiment were wearing brightly colored handkerchiefs fashioned of silk around their necks. These neck cloths, which probably descended from the Roman *fascalia* worn by orators to warm the vocal chords, struck the fancy of the king, and he soon made them an insignia of royalty as he created a regiment of Royal Cravattes. The word "cravat," incidentally, is derived from the word "Croat."

It wasn't long before this new style crossed the channel to England. Soon no gentleman would have considered himself well-dressed without sporting some sort of cloth around his neck—the more decorative, the better. At times, cravats were worn so high that a man could not move his head without turning his whole body. There were even reports of cravats worn so thick that they stopped sword thrusts. The various styles knew no bounds, as cravats of tasseled strings, plaid scarves, tufts and bows of ribbon, lace, and embroidered linen all had their staunch adherents. Nearly one hundred different knots were recognized, and as a certain M. Le Blanc, who instructed men in the fine and sometimes complex art of tying a tie, noted, "The grossest insult that can be offered to a man *comme il faut* is to seize him by the cravat; in this place blood only can wash out the stain upon the honor of either party."

In this country, ties were also an integral part of a man's wardrobe. However, until the time of the Civil War, most ties were imported from the Continent. Gradually, though, the industry gained ground, to the point that at the beginning of the twentieth century, American neckwear finally began to rival that of Europe, despite the fact that European fabrics were still being heavily imported.

In the 1960s, in the midst of the Peacock Revolution, there was a definite lapse in the inclination of men to wear ties, as a result of the rebellion against both tradition and the formality of dress. But by the mid-1970s, this trend had reversed itself to the point where now, in the 1980s, the sale of neckwear is probably as strong if not stronger than it has ever been.

How to account for the continued popularity of neckties? For years, fashion historians and sociologists predicted their demise—the one element of a man's attire with no obvious function. Perhaps they are merely part of an inherited tradition. As long as world and business leaders continue to wear ties, the young executives will follow suit and ties will remain a key to the boardroom. On the other hand, there does seem to be some aesthetic value in wearing a tie. In addition to covering the buttons of the shirt and giving emphasis to the verticality of a man's body (in much the same way that the buttons on a military uniform do), it adds a sense of luxury and richness, color and texture, to the austerity of the dress shirt and business suit.

Perhaps no other item of a man's wardrobe has altered its shape so often as the tie. It seems that the first question fashion writers always ask is, "Will men's ties be wider or narrower this year?"

In the late 1960s and early '70s, ties grew to five inches in width. At the time, the rationale was that these wide ties were in proportion to the wider jacket lapels and longer shirt collars. This was the correct approach, since these elements should always be in balance. But once these exaggerated proportions were discarded, fat ties became another victim of fashion.

The proper width of a tie, and one that will never be out of style, is 3¼ inches (2¾ to 3½ inches are also acceptable). As long as the proportions of men's clothing remain true to a man's body shape, this width will set the proper balance. Though many of the neckties sold today are cut in these widths, the section of the tie where the knot is made has remained thick—a holdover from the fat, napkinlike ties of the 1960s. This makes tying a small, elegant knot more difficult. Yet the relationship of a tie's knot to the shirt collar is an important consideration. If the relationship is proper, the knot will never be so large that it spreads the collar or forces it open, nor will it be so small that it will become lost in the collar.

Standard neckties come in lengths anywhere from 52 to 58 inches long. Taller men, or those who use a Windsor knot, may require a longer tie, which can be special-ordered. After being tied, the tips of the necktie should be long enough to reach the waistband of the trousers. (The ends of the tie should either be equal, or the smaller one just a fraction shorter.)

After you've confirmed the appropriateness of a tie's shape, next feel the fabric. If it's made of silk and it feels rough to the touch, then the silk is of an inferior quality. Silk that is not supple is very much like hair that's been dyed too often. It's brittle and its ends will fray easily. If care hasn't been taken in the inspection of ties, you may find misweaves and puckers.

All fine ties are cut on the bias, which means they have been cut across the fabric. This allows them to fall straight after the knot has been tied, without curling. A simple test consists of holding a tie across your hand. If it begins to twirl in the air, it was probably not cut on the bias and it should not be purchased.

Quality neckties want you to see everything: they have nothing to hide. Originally, neckties were cut from a single large square of silk, which was then folded seven times in order to give the tie a rich fullness. Today the price of silk and the lack of skilled artisans prohibits this form of manufacture. Ties now derive their body and fullness by means of an additional inner lining.

Besides giving body to the tie, the lining helps the tie hold its shape. The finest-quality ties today are lined with 100 percent wool and are generally made only in Europe. Most other quality ties use a wool mixture. The finer the tie, the higher the wool content. You can actually check. Fine linings are marked with a series of gold bars which are visible if you open up the back of the tie. The more bars, the heavier the lining. Many people assume that a quality tie must be thick, as this would suggest that the silk is heavy and therefore expensive. In fact, in most cases it is simply the insertion of a heavier lining that gives the tie this bulk. Be sure, then, that the bulk of the tie that you're feeling is the silk outer fabric and not the lining.

After you've examined the lining, take a look at the tie just above the spot where the two sides come together to form an inverted **V**. In most quality ties, you will find a stitch joining the back flaps. This is called the bar tack, and it helps maintain the shape of the tie.

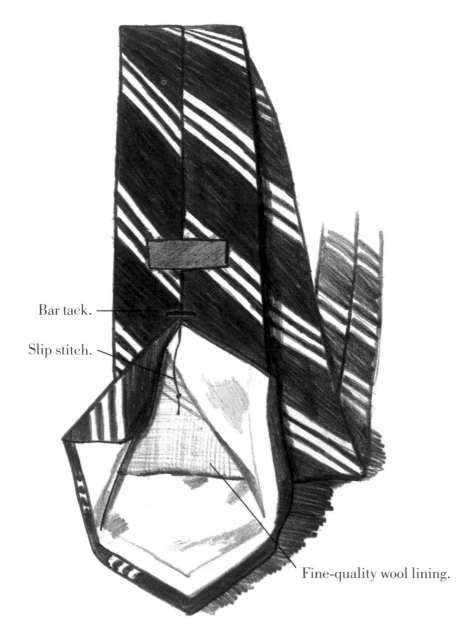

Bar tack.

Slip stitch.

Fine-quality wool lining.

Now, if you can, open up the tie as far as possible and look for a loose black thread. This thread is called the slip stitch and was invented by a man named Joss Langsdorf in the 1920s to give added resilience to the tie. The fact that the tie can move along this thread means that it won't rip when it's being wrapped tightly around your neck, and that it will, when removed, return to its original shape. Pull the slip stitch, and the tie should gather. If you can do this, you've found a quality, handmade tie.

Finally, take the tie in your hand and run your finger down its length. You should find three separate pieces of fabric stitched together, not two, as in most commercial ties. This construction is used to help the tie conform easily to the neck.

NECKTIE KNOTS

There are several standard ways to knot a tie: the four-in-hand knot (which dates back to the days of the coach and four in England, when the men on top of the coach would knot their ties in this manner to prevent them from flying in the wind while they were driving); the Windsor knot, purportedly invented by the Duke of Windsor, though he later disclaimed the invention; and the half-Windsor.

Though many men considered good dressers use the Windsor or half-Windsor knot, it has always struck me as giving too bulbous an appearance. For the most part, the majority of men simply do not look good wearing this knot, though there are a few notable exceptions, particularly Douglas Fairbanks, Jr. In any case, the Windsor knot only looks good when worn with a spread collar, which is how the Duke of Windsor originally wore it. My preference remains for the standard four-in-hand knot. It is the smallest and most precise of knots, and it has been the staple of the natural-shouldered, British-American style of dress in this country and in England for the past fifty years.

But whether one chooses the four-in-hand, the Windsor, or the half-Windsor, each should be tied so that there is a dimple or crease in the center of the tie just below the knot. This forces the tie to billow and creates a fullness that is the secret to its proper draping.

Tying the four-in-hand knot.

Tying the half-Windsor knot.

Tying the full-Windsor knot.

The tie on the left, lying flat against the
shirt, appears lifeless and dull, while in
the drawing on the right, the tie has
been properly arched, heightening its
visual interest.

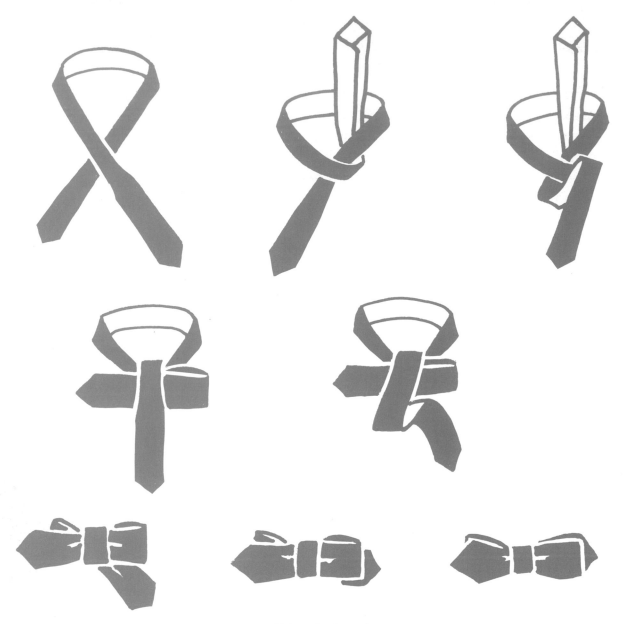

Tying the bow tie.

BOW TIES

The bow tie is derived from the stock worn several centuries ago. Stocks were made of washable fabrics and were wrapped many times around the neck and then tied in front. Eventually, this evolved into the single band around the neck, with the ends tied up in a bowlike configuration.

Recently, bow ties have enjoyed a renaissance. Worn for formal wear with a pleated-front shirt, they are appropriate and elegant. Worn during the day, they will give a man a casual or professorial look.

Bow ties should also avoid the extreme proportions. Tiny bows look just as silly and out of place as those huge butterflies that make men look as if their necks have been gift-wrapped. The general rule of thumb states that bow ties should never be broader than the widest part of the neck and should never extend beyond the outside of the points of the collar.

There are two classic shapes of bow ties: the butterfly (*near right*) and the bat wing.

TIE CARE

Ties are the most perishable item in a man's wardrobe, and as such they should be cared for appropriately. The proper care of your neckties actually begins when you take them off your neck. No matter how convenient it seems to slip the small end out of the knot, remember that you are significantly decreasing the longevity of the tie by using this method. Instead, untie the knot first, usually reversing the steps you used when you dressed in the morning. This reversal of steps will untwist the fibers of the material and lining and will help alleviate light creases. If creases are particularly severe, put the two ends of the tie together and roll the tie around your finger like a belt. Slip it off your finger and leave it rolled up overnight. The following morning, if it is a woven silk tie, hang it in your closet. Knitted or crocheted ties should not be hung but laid flat or rolled up instead and then placed in a drawer. This should return the tie to its original state.

Most experts agree that one ought not send a necktie out to be dry-cleaned. While dry cleaners may be able to remove spots, once they press the tie, they will compress the lining and dull the luster of the silk. A water stain can generally be removed by rubbing it with a piece of the same fabric (the other end of the tie, perhaps). More serious stains will often respond to a spot remover such as carbon tetrachloride. If none of this works, follow the example of Fred Astaire and turn your tie into a belt.

With proper care, your neckties can last almost forever. And if you've chosen them with a proper eye toward proportion, there's no reason you can't wear them at least as long as that.

FRED ASTAIRE—*A man who appreciated the value of a stylish pair of hose. Perhaps more than anyone else, he directed men's attention to their unlimited possibilities.*

V

Footwear and Hosiery

"Play not the peacock, looking everywhere about you to
see if you are well decked, if your shoes fit well, if your
stockings sit neatly, and your clothes handsomely."
—*GEORGE WASHINGTON, Rules of Courtesy and Decency of Behaviour*

It is entirely likely that prehistoric footwear consisted primarily of
tree bark, plant leaves, or animal hides tied around the bottom of
the foot simply to provide protection against rocks and rough terrain.
However, it wasn't long before footwear became a touch more
sophisticated while at the same time growing somewhat more
attractive, to the extent that, as with a hat, a man's status could be
judged merely on the basis of what he wore on his feet. In fact, many
relief paintings from Egyptian times depict fine-looking sandals of
interlacing palms and papyrus leaves worn by royalty along the order
of Tutankhamen.

Eventually leather, which is pliable, durable, and was easy
for man to obtain, became the dominant material used in footwear.
As it is a living substance and therefore breathes, it allows air to
circulate freely about the feet, adding appreciably to the comfort of
the wearer.

Historically, the lower classes continued to wear sandals
while those of higher position and rank chose to wear intricately
designed slippers. In the fifteenth, sixteenth, and seventeenth
centuries, when men's legs suddenly became a focal point of
fashion, shoes took on new importance, as highly decorated bows
and buckles were added to make them more attractive.

By the beginning of the nineteenth century, however, the
pendulum had begun to swing the other way, as shoes took on a
more functional look. Styles became rigid, almost clumsy; colors
vanished; and footwear was, for the most part, to be found only in
black and brown leathers.

In this country, Massachusetts quickly established itself as the shoemaking center of the Colonies. Thomas Beard, who settled in Salem soon after arriving on the *Mayflower* in 1629, is widely considered the pioneer of the American shoe industry. Following his lead, other craftsmen set up shop in many of the small towns surrounding Salem. The industry grew, and by 1768, nearly thirteen thousand pairs of shoes were being exported each year by Massachusetts shoemakers to the other Colonies.

Up until the middle of the nineteenth century, shoes were slowly and painstakingly produced by hand. But as soon as Elias Howe's sewing machine was adapted to the tasks of shoemaking, the industry began to join the Industrial Revolution.

In the meantime, footwear fashions ran the gamut from slippers to boots, which became popular in the early part of the nineteenth century. There were boots with spring heels, developed in 1835, and there were boots with no heels at all, popular in the middle part of the century. Boots began to fade from the scene somewhat just before the turn of the century, at about the same time that the rubber heel was first introduced.

During the first twenty-five years of this century, shoes were rather dull and lackluster. But by the time the 1930s rolled around footwear with more style and imagination began to make a long-awaited comeback. American manufacturers copied styles of English custom shoemakers, who were turning out new models every few months. Brogues became popular and once again color was added to footwear, with black-and-white "co-respondent" shoes (that is, shoes with contrasting colors). From the 1940s to the 1950s a wide variety of shoes existed, yet styles did not change much from year to year and one simply wore shoes until they were no longer in good enough condition to be worn any longer.

It wasn't until the 1960s and the advent of the Peacock Revolution that shoe fashion began to change radically, with new models introduced each season. The choices were mind-boggling: platform shoes; sleek, pointed English mod shoes of wild, iridescent colors; boots, from cowboy to hiking to frontier styles; and sneakers. Italian shoes—sleek and lightweight styles produced to go with the European cut suits—flooded the market and immediately became a favorite of the American man. Today the choice remains wide as to the kind of shoe a man can wear. There are men who wear practically nothing but sneakers or running shoes, while others enjoy the opportunity to change styles with each business and social engagement.

Hosiery, stockings, or leggings began simply as a binding or wrapping of the legs in order to provide protection. In Europe during the Middle Ages, people tied coarse cloth or skins around their legs, holding them up at the knees by the use of garters. By the eleventh century, when breeches were shortened to the knee, the lower leg was covered by a fitted cloth known as "chausses" or "hose" (probably derived from the Old English *hosa*).

At the time America was first colonized, early settlers were wearing heavy homespun woolen stockings in russets, blues, browns, and gray-greens. For the most part, styles in hosiery closely mirrored the styles being worn back in Europe, with the wealthier Colonial dressers able to afford hosiery of fine silk.

It wasn't until the early to middle nineteenth century, however, that knitting mills were established in this country, at which time the stocking industry found a home in several Connecticut towns. By this time, trousers had made their descent to just above the tops of the shoes, and as a result, hose was shortened accordingly. Over the next few decades, due to a need for extra warmth and comfort, hose length extended up, over the calf of the leg, and became known as the "sock" (probably from the Latin *soccus*, which was a light covering for the foot).

It was not until the twentieth century, though, that the hosiery industry began to flourish, as cotton, wool, and combinations of these fabrics in vivid colors and patterns caught the fashionable man's fancy. It was also during this period that sports hose in knitted wool, mixtures of wool and silk, and wool and cotton gained in popularity. This interest in patterns continued until the 1950s, at which time synthetic yarn for hosiery was introduced, permitting the manufacture of stretch hosiery, one-size-fits-all. Retailers, pleased to be able to reduce their inventory, didn't care that the hose was producible only in solid colors. Combined with the newfound interest in patterned trousers, solid hose regained popularity and fancy hose faded from the fashion scene. The industry has yet to recover. While today more patterns and colors are available for sports hosiery, a man looking for stylish dress hosiery has his work cut out for him.

Shoes are perhaps the most functional item in a man's wardrobe. And yet, in addition to serving a utilitarian purpose, shoes can often be the most obvious sign of a man's sense of style and social position.

As George Frazier often remarked, "Wanna know if a guy is well-dressed? Look down." And as Diana Vreeland, Frazier's counterpart in the women's fashion world and special consultant to the Metropolitan Museum's Costume Institute, advises concerning the development of a wardrobe: "First, I'd put money into shoes. No variety, just something I could wear with everything . . . . Whatever it is you wear, I think shoes are terribly important."

And they are. They reveal a good deal about the person wearing them. A man who buys fine leather shoes today shows that he respects quality, that he has confidence in his taste and in his future. Like other items of quality apparel, a well-made pair of shoes will give years of fine service if they are properly cared for. They must be of a design, however, that remains stylish through the years.

QUALITY SHOES

The key to a quality shoe is the way it's made and what it's made of. Eric Lobb, the great-grandson of the legendary English bootmaker John Lobb, discusses the criteria that go into the construction of a well-made shoe in his book *The Last Must Come First*. The last is the wooden form around which a shoe is made; hence it also determines the shape of the shoe itself. Lobb's pun, which was directed at the art of custom shoemaking, is actually a good guide for buying ready-made shoes. Examine first the last, or the shape of the shoe.

The shape of a shoe should follow as closely as possible the actual shape of one's own foot. The foot is not a particularly attractive feature of the anatomy, and a well-styled shoe will work to diminish its ungainliness by making it appear sleek and smaller. Think of the way a glove fits the hand: there are no excess bulges or gaps. A shoe should be cut similarly: no bulbous toes or crevices in front, a smooth line of leather following closely along the instep down to the edge of the toe. A custom-made shoe is designed to follow the shape of the foot so closely that the outside line and sole are curved (like the foot), while the inside, instead of being symmetrical, follows an almost straight line. A last of this sort in a ready-made shoe is a sign of elegance and knowledge on the part of the manufacturer.

The sole must also work to lighten the effect of the shoe. A heavy weighted sole or double soles on a shoe make the foot appear thick and inelegant. The double-soled shoes that many businessmen wear today, either in a heavy-grain leather or with wing-tip perforations, were marketed after World War II by manufacturers who based their design on army issue. These shoes really seem more appropriate for storming an enemy camp than for strolling along a city street. Look for a shoe with a sole no thicker than one-quarter inch. The heels should be low and follow the line of the shoe; they should not be designed as lifts. Most important, both sole and heel should be clipped close to the edge of the shoe with no obvious welt around the outside. Used chiefly for fine-quality wing-tips, cap-toes, and brogues, the welt is that narrow strip of leather stitched to the shoe upper and insole. The sole of the shoe is stitched to the welt, which gives the shoe a sturdiness and allows it to be resoled. In less expensive shoes, the sole is cemented to the upper. The sole's function is simply protection and support. It should not interfere with the shoe's shape or be overly visible.

The vamp is what one sees most on a shoe. It is the piece of leather that covers the top of the foot. By keeping this piece of leather low on the instep (a short vamp), the front of the shoe will appear shorter, making the entire foot seem smaller. This deaccentuation of length gives the foot a sleeker look. Naturally, the vamp should not be cut so low that the shoe can easily fall off.

In sum, a man should look to purchase only those shoes that have a small, well-shaped toe; thin, closely clipped soles and heels; and a vamp that is short enough to maintain a refined look.

CHOOSING THE RIGHT SHOE

The most important factor involved in the choice of a man's shoe besides fit is its appropriateness to the style of clothing he is wearing. The finest makers of shoes today are the English and the

Italians, but for the updated American style of dress, only the English-style shoes (though they may be made in either Italy or America) should be worn. This is so for two good reasons. First, the shape of the updated American-style clothing is on the fuller side, and thus the shoe ought to be on the fuller side as well, if for no other reason than that of balance. Also, the updated American-style clothing uses fabric of greater weight and texture, and it is therefore necessary that the shoe correspond to these elements. Italian shoes are trim-lined and lightweight, made to go with the European-cut suit, and as a result are totally inappropriate to the American style of dress.

The Italian ready-to-wear men's shoe industry began as an offshoot of the women's industry. It brought with it an interest in lightness, softness, and color, criteria that have always ruled the women's market. The fine calfskin uppers are glued to the leather soles with no welts and no inner soles to encumber the sleek look. They are made almost completely by hand with a craftsmanship and finesse that is unequaled elsewhere.

On the other hand, the British men's shoe industry came into its own immediately following the end of World War I, with the companies that had made army boots turning to the commercial marketplace to make up for the loss of their military contracts. The qualities of strength and durability that had made their boots legendary during the war were now built into shoes for the consumer. Unlike people in Italy, where the climate is generally dry and warm, the English have always had to contend with the worst elements of rain and cold. Their shoes were thus constructed of heavier skin that was not glued to the sole but sewn with a leather welt. British manufacturers, moreover, inserted a second leather sole—a middle sole between the outer sole and the inner—to make the shoes even more durable. All this interest in protection and durability gives the British shoe and its American offspring a fuller, more solid and substantial, look—the perfect balance for the updated American style of clothing.

This is not to advocate heavy, cloddy shoes, however. To the contrary: shoes should look neither too heavy nor too light. Nor should the style and color make them look too contrived. Trying to match the color of the shoes to the color of the suit is a woman's concept that has no place in the boardroom. A man's business shoe should never be a lighter shade than that of the suit; black or medium to dark brown have always and will continue to offer the proper balance to the business suit. As for shoe styles, there are approximately seven that tradition and good taste dictate as appropriate for business wear, and a man concerned with taste and style would do well to choose from among them.

The plain cap-toe brogue.

The Cap-Toe Brogue

The cap-toe, either plain or with a medallion decoration, is the most dressy business shoe one can wear, and for years this shoe has been the staple of the businessman's wardrobe. This lace-up shoe comes in black and various shades of brown. It is to be worn only with business suits of worsteds or flannels. In Boston it is considered perfectly proper to wear a highly polished brown version of this shoe with a navy suit, whereas in London it would be construed to be in poor taste to wear this combination.

The perforated cap-toe brogue.

The Wing-Tip Shoe

The traditional wing-tip or brogue shoe is a fine alternative to either the plain or the medallion cap-toe. It should be worn only in black, brown, or cordovan, and because of its heavy broguing, its wear can be expanded to include suits made with more textured fabrics, such as tweeds, cheviots, and flannels.

The wing-tip brogue.

The Slip-On Shoe or Dress Loafer

Slip-ons or Loafers have practically taken over the shoe industry because young men appreciate the convenience they offer. Yet much of what is worn today is of Italian style derivation and is much too sleek and lightweight for American-style suits. The simple slip-on, designed with understatement and using the shape and a version of the toe detail of the cap-toe or wing-tip style, should in no way be confused with the Gucci-style Loafer, for instance. This style shoe, with its identifiable gold or silver buckle, is far too casual and is thus inappropriate to be worn with the dressy business suit.

The dress slip-on.

The Monk-Strap Shoe

The monk-strap is a plain-toed, side-buckled shoe whose design was originally European. It is available in black or brown calf or chocolate-brown suede. Its plain front balances the sportiness of its design, thus giving it a wide range of sartorial applications. First popularized in the 1930s by European custom shoemakers, it is for the man who appreciates a little extra panache. The suede version made by Church is an enduring classic.

The calf monk-strap shoe.

The Suede Shoe

Until the Duke of Windsor, suede shoes were considered proper only for country attire. Once he took them to town, however, men immediately recognized the kind of soft elegance a suede shoe could offer in juxtaposition with the severe worsted suit. It remains the most elegant accompaniment to the business suit. The suede tie-up—either a wing-tip or cap-toe—offers practically limitless versatility, for it is a proper complement to as wide a range of wear as that encompassed by a seersucker suit to a sharkskin worsted, in any color from gray to green, in any season. Needless to say, it is probably not the shoe to wear in a stuffy bank atmosphere, or in a drenching spring downpour. But with these exceptions, there is probably no other shoe that can play so many roles in a man's wardrobe.

The suede cap-toe.

The Tassel Loafer

This originally sporty shoe has gained increasing acceptance as a shoe appropriate for business wear. The push has come from Americans' growing penchant for sporty comfort rather than proper styles. The black tassel Loafer—originally popular with the Ivy League set in the 1920s—offers about the same level of dressiness as the blue blazer, which itself falls on a somewhat ambiguous line between the business suit and the sports jacket. Thus, any place the blazer is not quite right, this shoe is not either. Brown tassel Loafers are even more sporty, with cordovan somewhere in between brown and black. There is probably no shoe (except perhaps the white buck) that has more identity as an American shoe than the tassel Loafer. It remains a lovely, casual shoe, the kinetic motion of its tassel projecting a jaunty sense of well-being. But still, it should not be confused with proper business footwear.

The tassel Loafer.

Summer Shoes

Today most men choose to wear their brogue business shoes twelve months a year and are quite correct to do so. However, for those who prefer a change of tempo when the summer months arrive and their seersucker or cotton suits come out of the closet, there are some alternatives. These include the cap-toe or wing-tip shoe in medium brown calf or suede; the classic white buck lace-up with red rubber soles; and the black-and-white or brown-and-white suede and leather co-respondent shoe. Unfortunately, the co-respondent shoe, perhaps the height of summer elegance, is difficult to find today in an acceptable version that uses white buckskin instead of the heavier thick suede or imitation leather. While there is the temptation in summer to wear a lighter-colored shoe, none of these look well with dark business suits. The principle that a similarity of tone ought to exist between the shoe and the suit should prevail even in summer. These lighter shoes are meant to be worn with the more mid-shade tropical worsteds and gabardines or the more casual poplins and seersuckers.

The white buck oxford.

FIT

From the time the government banned the use of X-ray machines, fitting a pair of shoes has become strictly a matter of feel. There are no real secrets in this regard. The size that feels comfortable for you is the size to choose. However, most men's feet are each of a slightly different size, and so one should buy the shoe to fit the larger foot, which means, of course, that both shoes should be tried on. Remember that certain soft leathers, particularly in Loafers, will stretch up to a half size. A good fit should allow one to wiggle one's toes while the heel fits snugly into the back of the shoe. There should be good support underneath the instep, and the shoe should be widest at the ball, where one's foot is the widest. Also, make sure there is enough room under the toe box so that there is no pressure on the top of your toes, and see that the insole is flat and extends to the shoe upper.

Shoes should feel comfortable from the moment you try them on. If they're not, it's highly unlikely that they will ever be "broken in" entirely to your liking.

CARE

The best way to care for a pair of leather shoes is to keep them polished and give them ample rest. Polish protects the leather from water and from scuffing. To clean leather, use a cream to lift the dirt and then follow with a wax to protect and polish the shoe.

Many men buy new shoes and are so eager to wear them that they forget to rub on a first coat of polish. This pre-conditioning of the leather will increase the shoe's resistance to dirt and water and is perhaps the most important first step in preventative maintenance.

Leather absorbs moisture. This is what allows it to stretch and why it is so important for shoes to be given time to rest. Never wear a pair of shoes for more than one day at a time. Leather breathes like cotton or wool. It needs at least a day or two to dry out, in order to release trapped moisture (if your shoes do get wet, be sure and keep them away from sources of excessive heat, such as a radiator), and to return to its original shape. By alternating shoes and keeping shoe trees in them, there is no limit on the years they can last. But if shoes are worn day after day and especially if they have not been adequately polished, the skin becomes moldy and attenuated until finally the suppleness disappears and the leather begins to crack. Leather is a skin. Treat it with the same respect and care you give your own.

If you have suede shoes, they can best be cleaned with a suede brush or artist's gum eraser. However, you should be careful not to over-rub, as this will destroy the nap of the suede.

It is best to keep shoes in constant repair. Worn heels will throw one's whole body out of alignment and cause the shoe to stretch out of shape. Shoes should be reheeled and resoled as soon as this appears to be required.

THE FINER POINTS

Skins

It is the skin used in the upper part of the shoe that more than any other factor determines the quality and cost of that particular shoe. The softer, more supple the leather, the higher the quality. Supple leather will last longer, as it does not easily crack. Such leather generally comes from smaller animals—kids and calves—which means there is less of it; hence its higher cost.

Calfskin is leather made from the hide of young cattle. It is lightweight, supple and fine-grained, and is generally used for quality business shoes. Cowhide is somewhat heavier than calfskin. It can be grained, embossed, or finished to enhance its natural texture and is generally found in casual shoes and boots. Kidskin is made from the skin of young goats. It is soft and light and is generally used for dress and tailored slip-ons. Suede is leather that is finished on the flesh side of the skin in order to produce a nap. The finest suede today is made from the male deer (buckskin). Cordovan is leather from the rump of a horse, and it is distinguished by its red-brown color. It is perhaps the most durable of all leathers. Patent leather has a synthetic surface that produces a glossy finish, and it is used mostly for dressy, evening shoes.

Before purchasing a shoe, feel the leather. Bend the shoe and watch how the leather moves. It should be soft and flexible and return quickly to its original shape.

Soles and Linings

The surest marks of a fine-quality shoe are leather soles and heels and leather linings within the shoe. It is said that a man exerts as much pressure on the soles of his feet when walking as an elephant does. Whether or not this is completely accurate, the pressure per square inch is nevertheless enormous. The sole provides a kind of shock absorber, and good leather does this better than almost any other material. A leather heel provides further cushioning with just enough give to make walking pleasant. Rubber soles can also cushion but because they will not slide on pavement, friction is built up when walking. Over a period of time, this can make your feet feel hot and uncomfortable.

Inside the shoe, the extra layer of leather that covers the interior offers further protection from the cold and gives greater structural support to the shoe. It also increases the shoe's life span. Aesthetically, a leather inner lining is a handsome detail that separates the fine quality shoe from the mass market model.

The Waist

The waist is the narrow part of the last where the front and back of the shoe come together under the instep. Like the vamp, a small waist can be helpful in creating the appearance of a more elegant shoe. Instead of having a blocky look, a small-waisted shoe curves smoothly in and then out, giving a cleaner, more streamlined look.

Vamp Decorations

Loafers with buckles or chains across the vamp have become increasingly popular since the Gucci Loafer was first marketed in the United States in the mid-1960s. One should be careful not to allow these gold or silver decorations to become so large or gaudy that they destroy the integrity of a man's look by drawing immediate attention to his shoes. More effective as vamp decorations are the leather penny saddle (Weejun shoe) or tassels. These work to break up the vamp, thus making it and the shoe look smaller and finer. And yet, because they are made of the same color leather as the shoe, they are not so obvious as to attract attention.

HOSIERY

A pair of hose is meant to keep your feet warm and to prevent irritation from rubbing shoes. This, of course, is the most basic definition of a pair of hose. They can do much more, however. Wear black hose with a dark blue suit, and they only serve their pragmatic purpose. But put on a pair of burgundy wool hose, and suddenly you've created aesthetic interest where none previously existed. Instead of a splash of color just at the top of the suit where the tie and handkerchief fall, you now have a subtle response at the bottom.

As a general principle, the dressier the clothing one is wearing, the finer the hose should be. This ranges from sheer silk or cotton lisle in formal wear, to fine ribbed wool or cotton in business wear, to cashmere or wool argyles for sports jackets and odd trousers. The hose should reflect the level of formality of the suit. One doesn't wear argyle socks with a pin-striped worsted, nor would one wear fine cotton lisle with a Harris tweed sports jacket.

The best type of hose is that made from natural fibers— cotton or wool. These materials allow a better flow of air, cutting down on perspiration and heat. When they are thin, as they should be, they are naturally delicate. However, because of the introduction of nylon reinforced heels and toes, your hose should serve you a reasonable length of time.

The length of hose ought to be either calf height or above the calf. Ankle-high hose are definitely to be avoided. Nothing looks worse when a man's legs are crossed than an exposed patch of skin separating the top of his hose and the trouser bottoms. The surest antidote is above-calf hose or calf-high socks worn with garters. While garters may sound like a bother, they do keep up one's hose and free one from having to wear high socks, thus eliminating their stockinglike sensation.

Good dressing dictates that the color of hose (or one of the predominant colors in their pattern) should relate to something above the waist, such as a tie, shirt, or handkerchief, with the hose always on the darker side of that color. Generally, the best dressers try to do something a little special with their hose. Anyone, they figure, can wear hose that match his trousers. They look for hose with interesting colors and patterns. Unfortunately, the wonderful clockface French lisle hose of the 1940s and '50s are nearly extinct, as are the fine-gauged ribbed English wool embroidered hose. Still, with a little enterprise, one can find a fine two- or three-color bird's-eye or other subtle pattern that will accomplish the same end. In these cases, the accent color of the pattern ought to relate to something above the waist.

Though the easy way out may be merely to stick to plain blue or black, why not try a medium gray wool with a dark suit? Or perhaps burgundy, or even a subtle pattern? It won't only be your feet that will enjoy the change.

VI

Accessories:
Suspenders, Belts,
Handkerchiefs, and Jewelry

"Correspondences are like small-clothes before the invention of suspenders; it is impossible to keep them up."

—*SYDNEY SMITH*

From the time man first chose to wear trousers, either leather belts, rope, or cloth sashes were used to hold them up. It wasn't until the time of the French Revolution, however, when short vests and trousers reaching to the armpits were worn, that the suspender first appeared. These early examples were merely straps of leather that fell directly over the shoulders and were fastened to the waistband of the trousers by means of a hook.

Within a short time, suspenders, which were originally quite heavy and rather uncomfortable, became the favored choice of nobility and were eventually considered the mark of any well-dressed gentleman. In fact, no properly attired Victorian man would have dared consider himself affianced to any young woman of breeding until she had presented him with a pair of suspenders embroidered by her own dainty hands.

In this country, suspenders were also considered the only choice of the well-dressed man, but by the end of the nineteenth century, this thinking began to undergo a slow yet inexorable change. This change was due, at least in part, to the uniforms men wore during the various wars that flared up during the late nineteenth century. Belts became more popular as shoulders were emphasized and waists pulled in, simply in an effort to appear more threatening and imposing.

109

By the early 1900s, folded belts were all the rage. They were fashioned by joining two ½-inch strips of cowhide, then stitching the edges to produce a rounded, pliable belt one inch in width. Also popular during this period was the Sam Browne officer's belt, which appealed not only to veterans but to other men as well.

But it was probably S. Rae Hickock, a successful dealer in leather goods, who did more than anyone to ensure the success of the belt industry when he began to manufacture belt buckles with etched monograms around 1910.

By the time American men returned home from World War I, they were wearing coarse yarn belts, which quickly caught the fancy of the general male populace. However, during the summer, when vests and jackets came off, belts went on as men chose not to expose their suspenders. Also during this period knickers became popular, further limiting the use of suspenders. And although suspenders maintained their popularity well into the decade of the 1920s, by the time the stock market fell, most men's trousers were being held up by belts.

Though they have recently experienced a renaissance of sorts, today suspenders are but a small part of the haberdashery industry. Belts, on the other hand, come in many colors, widths, and all sorts of materials, ranging from leather to fabric to plastic.

The first handkerchief, probably used either to cover the head or to wipe perspiration from the face, was made of small mats of woven grass. However, the first handkerchief solely for the face was used in conjunction with religion. These early handkerchiefs, called "facials," were simply small pieces of silk tissue used by priests at the altar and then left there when the service was completed.

In early times the handkerchief functioned both as a utilitarian accessory and as a showy dress item, carried in the hand as opposed to being tucked into a pocket. By the time of the early Renaissance, handkerchiefs were considered an essential accessory, prompting Erasmus to note that "To wipe your nose on your sleeve is boorish." Soon handkerchiefs became more ornate, at which point they also began to serve as tokens of a man's love for a woman, and vice versa.

By the turn of this century, handkerchiefs made of silk,

linen, or cotton were de rigueur for the breast pocket of a gentleman's suit jacket, and he could not be considered properly dressed without one. Of course, during the 1960s most men eschewed handkerchiefs in their breast pockets, but today—as in the 1930s—they are still the choice of the well-dressed gentleman.

For the most part, a man's jewelry has always been utilitarian in nature, though this is by no means to say that it has not always been worn with an eye toward personal adornment.

Those of wealth and nobility were, of course, the ones who naturally gravitated toward jewelry, including rings, shirt studs, various kinds of pins, and, recently, wristwatches, tie bars, cufflinks, and collar bars. Of all these, it is the wristwatch that is the most modern. Said to originate with the French, it came into vogue during World War I, when it was worn by soldiers in the trenches.

Today a man has several choices as to the kind of jewelry he can wear, jewelry that should relate to his style of dress. It is possible to select jewelry that enhances one's appearance while at the same time serving a practical function.

Many men feel that once they have selected the proper suit, shirt, and tie, the other accessories can be added with little further consideration. Yet the fact is, the use of a handkerchief or jewelry can subtly alter the mood or entire effect of the ensemble. Besides, where one must be somewhat conservative in one's choice of suit, shirt, and shoes in order to be properly dressed, the choice of suspenders or belt, handkerchiefs, or suitable jewelry allows a welcome freedom.

SUSPENDERS AND BELTS

At least from the turn of this century suspenders have been identified with business wear while belts were considered an accoutrement of sports clothing. There are several practical reasons why suspenders are still the proper choice to be worn with the business suit, especially one with pleated trousers. Suspenders permit the trousers to hang best, supporting the front of the pants as well as the rear. They allow the pleat to establish its proper line and make the crease of the trousers more apparent. Additionally, suspenders are more comfortable than belts, which must be drawn tight around the waist in order to hold up the trousers. With suspenders, trousers can be worn loosely around the body, the only contact one feels coming at the point where the suspenders cross the shoulders. One might also note that during the summer months the wearing of suspenders actually promotes a certain coolness, as the roominess of the trousers around the waist area makes for improved air circulation.

Suspenders also have the added advantage of allowing the length of the trousers to remain constant. Normally, a man's trousers stretch at the waistband during the course of a day. Suspenders eliminate the need to pull them up two, three, four, or more times a day. For all these reasons and more, suspenders will always remain preferable to belts in dress wear.

Frankly, there is simply no place for belts in the realm of tailored clothing. They cut a man's body in half, interrupting the smooth transition of the suit from shoulders to trouser cuffs. And they are particularly disruptive when one is wearing a vested suit. Either the belt creates a bulge under the vest or else it sticks out beneath it, completely destroying the line.

Today the finest suspenders are made of rayon, replacing yesteryear's silk. Produced only in England but available in America, they come with leather fittings and adjustable brass levers. (Elasticized suspenders are not a substitute; not only do they lack style, but they function poorly and are less comfortable.) The straps of most fine suspenders are cut in 1¼- or 1½-inch strips. Any smaller and they will bind; wider, they feel unnatural.

Trousers to be worn with suspenders should have two buttons in the back that are equidistant from the center of the fork of the suspenders. In front, there are four buttons: one over each of the main pleats, the other two just forward of the side seam. They may be sewn inside or outside the waistband, depending upon personal preference. Trousers should always be worn larger at the waist so that they are actually "suspended" from the shoulders.

Needless to say, belts should never be worn in conjunction with suspenders. It is considered in poor taste. Therefore, if the

The suspenders' single rear fitting is fastened to buttons on either side of the center seam.

Suspender tabs are fastened to buttons positioned above the forward pleats and just ahead of the trouser side seams. The brass levers will rest several inches above the leather fittings if the suspenders are the correct length.

trousers you're wearing are to be worn with suspenders, make sure your tailor removes the belt loops.

Perhaps the only person who might encounter some difficulty wearing suspenders is someone with sharply sloped shoulders. In such a case, the back fork of the suspenders can be raised to compensate. This may be accomplished simply by using the excess material from the hem of the trousers to make tabs that can be sewn to the back, thereby effectively raising the fork higher on the back, which in turn will keep the suspenders from sliding.

While almost all aspects of businesswear are designed to enhance the impression of seriousness of purpose on the part of the wearer, suspenders offer perhaps a singular opportunity to lighten up an austere image. There are no limits to the colors and patterns that are deemed acceptable. There are successful, serious men in the financial community who wear embroidered dollar-sign suspenders, and others who wear those embroidered with golf clubs or naked ladies. Against all vagaries of fashion, they have been doing it for years. No doubt they will continue to do so. When the opportunity is there, fine dressers make the most of it.

BELTS

Once again, it must be emphasized that belts are properly worn only with sports clothes. However, if one does choose to wear a belt with a business suit, it should be simple, with a small buckle that does not call attention to itself. The buckle can be made in either gold or silver color, generally matching the color of the jewelry one wears. If there are initials embossed on it, make sure they are your own and not some "designer's."

The belt itself should be between $\frac{7}{8}$ and $1\frac{1}{4}$ inches in width. Its color can relate either to the color of your suit or the shoes you are wearing. It should never be so long that the belt's extra piece overlaps more than a few inches past the first loop after it's buckled, nor should it be so short that it just barely makes it through the buckle.

Simplicity and understatement should be the keys to dress belts. Perhaps the most elegant belts are those of black or brown pin seal, lizard, or the ultimate in luxury, crocodile. All take a simple nonornamented gold or brass buckle.

HANDKERCHIEFS

The suit jacket is made with a left breast pocket not to hold a pack of cigarettes or a pair of glasses but to hold a handkerchief. Without one, an outside breast pocket appears to be an unnecessary detail, and a man looks as if he hasn't finished dressing.

A simple white handkerchief is all that is necessary to complete the business ensemble. It is also the least expensive way a man can quickly elevate his level of style. The handkerchief, like the hose, gives a man one more opportunity to do something a little out of the ordinary, something a bit more inventive. A white handkerchief placed in the breast pocket of a dark suit offers a touch of elegance and is a sure sign of a confident and knowledgeable dresser.

The finest white handkerchiefs are made of linen with hand-rolled edges. While they are difficult to find today, they are worth searching for. The virtue of linen is that because of its inherent stiffness, it retains its starched quality throughout the day. It is the only handkerchief fabric that looks as fresh in the evening as it did in the morning, when it was first folded.

While a white linen handkerchief is the easiest choice for many, since it is always proper, for those more adventuresome dressers, there are handkerchiefs in colors and patterns. In this case, it is generally the tie that is the determining factor in choosing the proper pocket square. The pocket square must complement the tie, though it should never directly match it in pattern or color. Some of the nicest colored handkerchiefs are made of linen in traditional Oxford shirting colors, or in pure white with colored borders. Another possibility is silk. These come in a wide array of solid colors. But instead of solids, wear silk in the traditional English ancient madder patterns, such as paisley or foulard. The colors in these are muted and give a more subtle effect.

If your tie is of silk, a handkerchief of a dry linen fabric looks best, while if your tie is of wool or cotton, silk in the breast pocket will add the proper textural balance to the chest area.

There are four ways to fold a handkerchief properly: square-ended, puffed, multi-pointed, and triangle fold. The multi-pointed and the triangle effect are certainly the most elegant and are for use with handkerchiefs of linen or cotton with hand-rolled edges. Silk handkerchiefs look better with the puffed method. The square end (or TV fold), a popular style in the 1940s and '50s, seems a little staid today. Yet whatever method is chosen, the placing of the handkerchief must not appear overly studied. The material should show above the pocket no more than an inch to an inch and a half.

The square-ended fold.

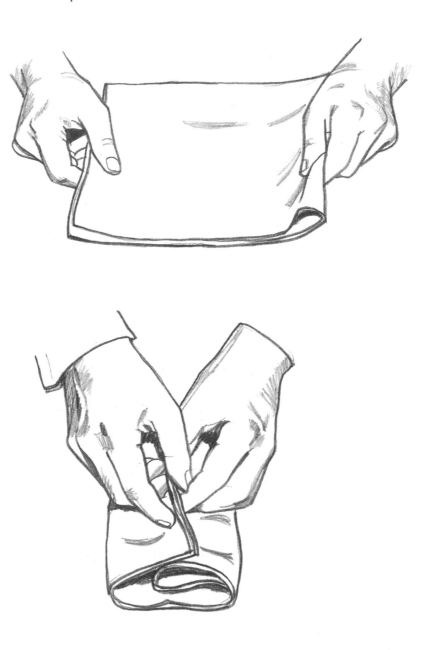

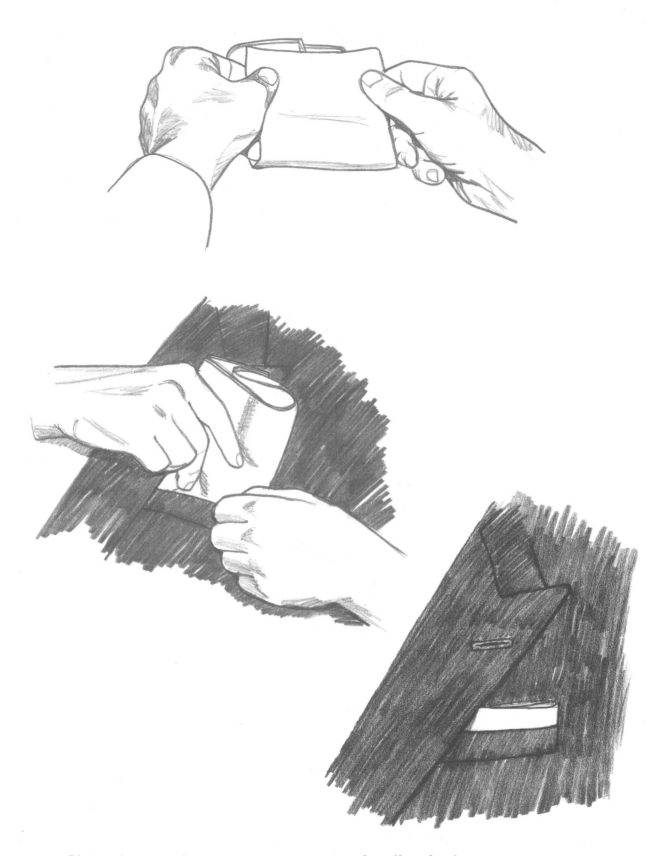

If you choose to have a monogram on your handkerchief,
never let it show.

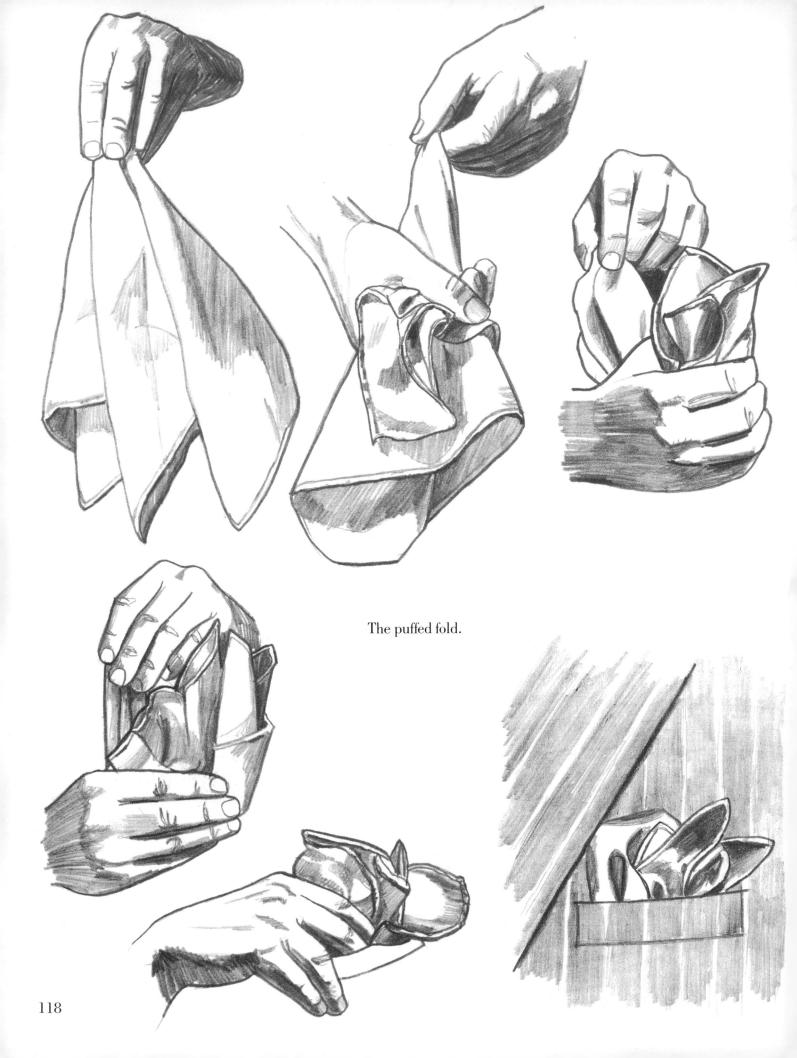

The puffed fold.

118

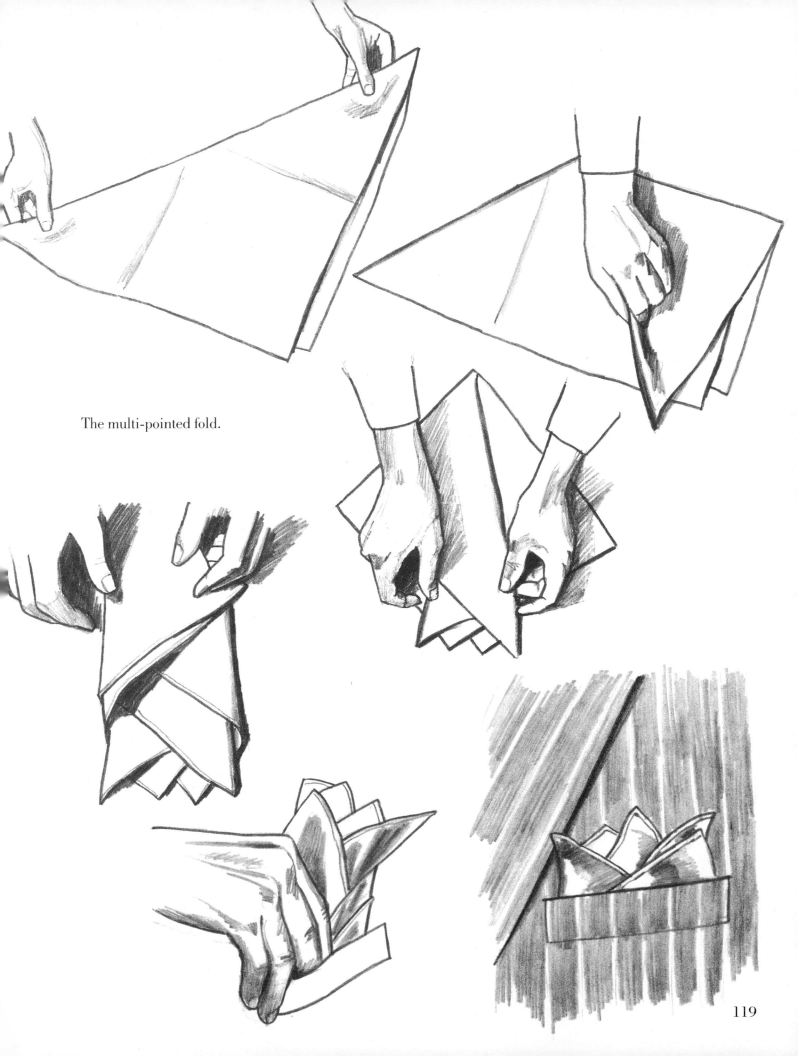

The multi-pointed fold.

119

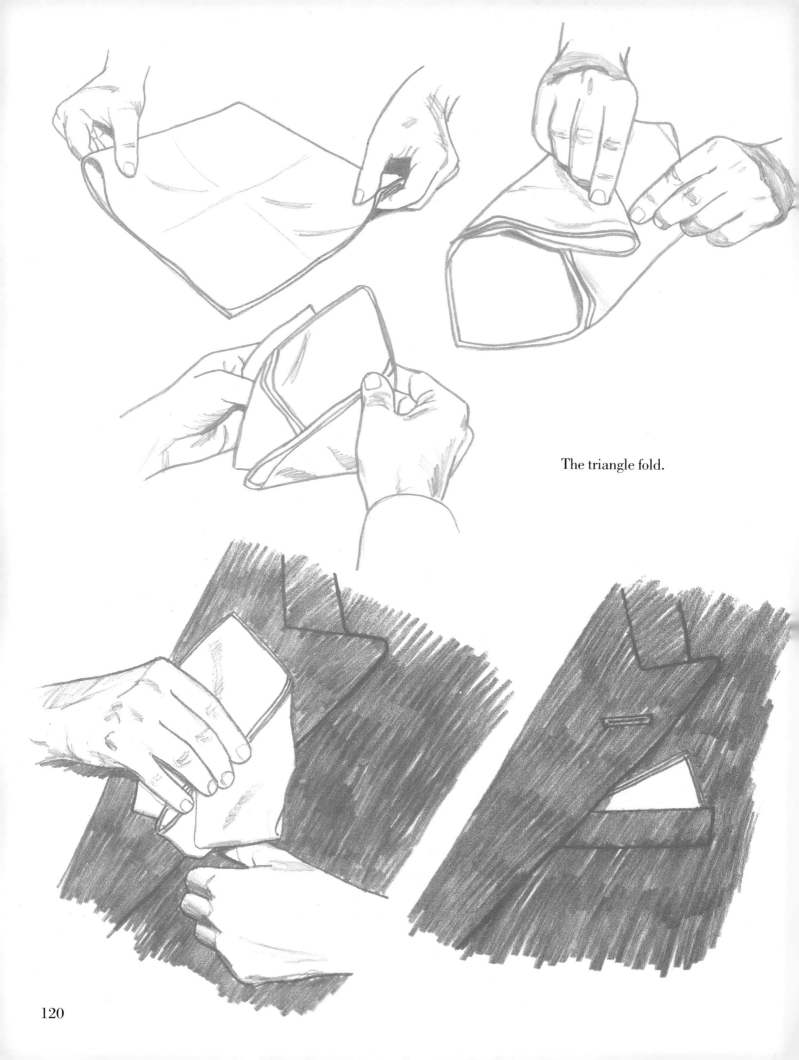

The triangle fold.

JEWELRY

For men who like jewelry, there is plenty of opportunity to wear it when one is dressing up. There are the collar bar, tie holder, cufflinks, watch or key chain, wristwatch, and ring. Almost all are functional, but each may add an element of elegance to the wearer. Men's jewelry looks best when simple. Leave Florentine gold to the women. Stay away from rococo and baroque designs. If you want to wear something a little different, do it with humor or whimsy, not ostentation. Try cufflinks in the shape of hearts, or perhaps a tie clip in the shape of a tie.

If you wear cufflinks, never choose those with a clip on one side. They look as if you could only afford the gold or jewel on the outside. The best-made cufflinks and the most elegant ones are those with matching sides. After all, cufflinks are supposed to link both sides of a French cuff, not clip them together.

If you choose to wear a collar bar, select one in a gold or silver safety-pin style. Contrary to popular notion, holes made by the pin in the collar will close up after the shirt is washed. The clip models occasionally have interesting designs but never hold securely to the collar edge and must be adjusted throughout the day. The bar with a ball on either end, one of which screws on and off for use, is also very smart. The shirt collar must have holes sewn specifically for this particular bar. When worn properly, this method of securing the collar is no doubt the most elegant.

The wearing of a tie holder is optional, but it certainly produces a neater, more controlled look. It should not, however, be large or gaudy. A narrow gold bar with a plain design or a small clip looks best. The clip should never dominate the tie or stand out. It should be placed in the bottom half of the tie at a forty-five-degree angle downward, adhering to the rule that nothing ought to cross the body directly.

The most elegant watches are those with thin faces, trimmed in gold. The thinner the watch, the dressier it is. If you choose a pocket watch, make sure the chain is long enough to create a natural curve.

As a general rule, the color of all jewelry a man wears ought to be the same. If your cufflinks are a gold color, then your collar bar should be the same. Unlike female jewelry, men's jewelry should never be the focal point of what is being worn. Its role is functional, and in this regard one might well adhere to a tenet of the architect Miës van der Rohe: "Less is more."

ADOLPHE MENJOU—*One of Hollywood's most elegant dressers.*

122

VII
Formal Wear

"Formal dress lifts a man out of the ordinary,
if he should be ordinary to begin with."

—*ROGER SMITH*

The notion of a man "dressing up" after the sun goes down, whether it be in top hat and tails or simply in his best finery, has been with us for centuries. In fact, in the great European opera houses of the eighteenth and nineteenth centuries, the "dress circle" meant just that, with no one allowed in unless he or she was properly attired.

However, the idea of wearing black for evening wear was, according to the English clothing historian James Laver, first introduced by the nineteenth-century British writer Edward Bulwer-Lytton, who utilized it "as a romantic gesture to show that he was a 'blighted being' and very, very melancholy."

And it was Bulwer-Lytton who gave further impetus to this notion of black as the color for formal wear by writing, in 1828, that "people must be very distinguished to look well in black." Naturally, the moment this statement was noted by would-be dandies, the style became decidedly de rigueur, and it wasn't long before black became popular for daytime wear as well.

Although for years white tie and tails were the traditional mode of formal attire, the introduction of the dinner jacket added another viable alternative from which the well-dressed gentleman could choose.

The original dinner jacket was simply an adaptation of the "Cowes" jacket—a sort of compromise between a mess jacket, a smoking jacket, and a dress coat—invented for or by King Edward VII when he was Prince of Wales, and worn by him first at dinner aboard his yacht at Cowes and then later at other semi-formal evening gatherings away from London. The original single-breasted model was simply a tailcoat without a tail, worn with white piqué vest and later with a matching black vest of the same fabric as the jacket and trousers.

The dinner jacket made its debut in the United States in 1896, when a celebrated dandy named Griswold Lorillard wore it to a white-tie-and-tails ball at an exclusive country club in Tuxedo Park, New York. Tuxedo Park, founded in the 1880s by a group of prominent and wealthy New Yorkers as a residential club colony, was an "informally formal" community. Apparently, society had had enough of tails, which had traditionally been worn for formal evening wear, because Lorillard's "invention" was immediately accepted in even the stuffiest of circles. The use of the term "tuxedo," sometimes lamentably abbreviated to "tuck," or, even worse, to "tux," is pretty much confined to the United States. The garment is known abroad, and generally in this country as well, by its correct name of "dinner jacket," or (frequently in the New York area) "dinner coat." It is probably seldom, if ever, called a "tuxedo" in Tuxedo Park.

The dinner jacket remained just as its inventor intended until the 1920s, when the next Prince of Wales—later to become the Duke of Windsor—ordered a new dinner jacket (by this time, Lorillard's tuxedo had taken the name of its American birthplace), and specifically requested that the fabric be not black, but blue —midnight blue, to be precise. Under artificial light, midnight blue appears black—blacker than black, in fact—whereas black, under the same artificial conditions, tends to take on a greenish cast. The new color caught on, and is now counted among the great sartorial inspirations of that bygone era.

In the 1930s, the prince once again tinkered with tradition, appearing in a double-breasted dinner jacket. Although the double-breasted dinner jacket was first ordered from a Savile Row tailor by the English song-and-dance man Jack Buchanan (who also wrote extensively on fashion), it was most certainly the prince who popularized this style. Worn with a soft-front pleated evening shirt, this innovation brought a new level of informality to the traditional dinner jacket—but with no lowering of the standards that separated those who dressed correctly from those who simply dressed up.

Throughout the remainder of the twentieth century, the tuxedo has undergone various stylistic changes, including the excesses characteristic of the decade of the sixties. And yet, fashion aside, the proper tuxedo, whether it be single- or double-breasted, still endures as the most elegant attire for any man.

For a man, no other form of dress is as steeped in such a ritualistic sense of propriety as formal wear. There is something so elegant about the simplicity of black and white, with its stark contrast and lack of pattern, that when the elements are properly put together, they present a man at his most debonair.

After dark or 6 p.m.—whichever arrives first—there are two ensembles that can properly be called formal: white tie, which means tails, or black tie, better known as the tuxedo.

The more formal of these ensembles is white tie, which includes a tailcoat with matching trousers trimmed by two lines of braid on the outside of each trouser leg, white piqué tie, white piqué single- or double-breasted waistcoat, and wing-collar shirt with stiff piqué front.

However, with the exception of a man's wedding day, or occasions of state, a man will probably never be called upon to wear white tie. Nevertheless, anyone residing in a city, large or small, will probably find himself attending affairs requiring black tie at least several times a year, as more and more people today are re-experiencing the pleasures of dressing up. Thus, a properly styled tuxedo is one of the smartest and potentially most enduring investments a man can make for his wardrobe. Unfortunately, though, like most solid investments, a fine tuxedo is not easy to find.

There are four proper styles for the tuxedo: the single- or double-breasted with a peaked lapel with grosgrain facing on the lapel, or the single- or double-breasted shawl collar with either satin or grosgrain on the lapel facings. These are the only proper choices.

Yet American manufacturers, in order to save on costs and increase profits, have taken to producing a notched lapel—the same style manufactured for their normal daytime suits—and facing them in satin. This unfortunate trend began in the sixties, when men were

The single-breasted peaked-lapel tuxedo.

experimenting with alternative styles of dress. Once manufacturers realized it was less costly to produce this model, they persisted. Today the man seeking a proper dinner jacket, with either peaked lapels or shawl collar, has his work cut out for him. One might try searching the better men's specialty stores, but even the venerated Brooks Brothers sells the notched style. The more adventuresome man can explore the second-hand shops. Or, finally, he can have his formal wear custom-made.

The most versatile jacket style is the single-breasted, peaked-lapel model. It was the original black-tie model, the direct descendant of the tailcoat, and its angular lapels look best with a wing collar, the tailcoat's original complement. It can be worn with a vest or cummerbund, and even with a turndown collar. Peaked lapels look equally elegant on the double-breasted version of this coat. The double-breasted model offers the advantage of allowing the wearer to dispense with a vest or cummerbund.

The shawl collar model, either single-breasted or double-breasted, has a more subtle look than the peaked-lapel models. Because of its Old World image and the fact that it is a jacket style worn only for evening wear, it is especially favored by the most sophisticated dressers. However, if one's build is on the portly or rotund side, one might want to avoid the shawl collar, as it tends to accentuate the roundness.

Both single- and double-breasted jackets are at their best either without vents or with moderate side vents. Whichever style one chooses, the pockets should never be in the flap style, which is traditionally associated with day wear.

The color should be black or, if one is lucky enough to unearth one in this color, midnight blue, in a finished or unfinished worsted. In summer or at a resort, a white or midnight-blue dinner jacket in a tropical-weight worsted is always correct.

Trousers

Tuxedo trousers follow rules identical with those applying to day wear. Made of the same fabric as the jacket, they should have a natural taper, following the shape of one's leg. The bottoms should be plain—never cuffed—and break just on top of the shoe. On each trouser leg, there should be a satin braid, a remnant of detail first introduced on military uniforms to cover the exposed outside seam.

The single-breasted shawl-collar tuxedo.

While plain-front trousers are more common, pleated trousers add a touch of elegance. If one chooses pleats, be certain that their folds open toward the center for proper fullness. In either case, the waistband must never be exposed. It is the job of the vest, the pleated cummerbund, or the closed double-breasted jacket to keep it hidden. And the recent invention of an all-in-one waistband-cum-cummerbund is simply no substitute for the real thing.

The Shirt

There are two proper shirt styles from which to choose. The more formal is a white winged-collar shirt with stiff piqué bosom and single cuffs (see the illustration on page 126). The second choice, less formal but decidedly more comfortable, is the turndown collar shirt with soft-pleated front and double French cuffs—yet another sartorial contribution of the Duke of Windsor. (See the illustration on the facing page.)

Wing-collar shirts look fine on a person who has a long neck, setting off the tie and framing the face, but they should be avoided by those with shorter necks. Though winged collars attached to shirts can now be purchased, the classic and still preferable alternatives, because of their stiffness, are the detachable-collar shirts. These detachable-collar shirts are sold all over London and, in this country, at Brooks Brothers.

Pleated-bosom shirts should be bought in fine cotton or, for the ultimate in luxury, a dull, eggshell-color, lustrous silk. For piqué-front shirts, the customary body fabrics are batiste, voile, or a light cambric. The finer the bead of the piqué, the finer and more elegant the shirt front.

A couple of fine points to remember: The pleated bosom or stiff front of the shirt should never extend below the waistband of the trousers, or the shirt will bow when you sit down or bend over. It is also a good idea to have a tab with a buttonhole sewn in the front of the shirt that can then be attached by a button to the waistband of your trousers. This will further prevent your shirt from billowing out over the cummerbund or vest.

Ideally, your shirt should have eyelets for studs, since buttons are properly worn for day wear. Piqué-front shirts take one or two eyelets, while soft fronts usually require two or three.

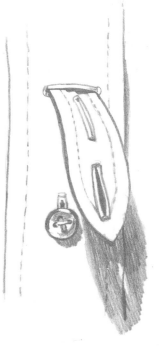

The tab attaches to the inside button on the waistband of the formal trouser. It prevents the shirt from riding up out of the trouser.

Vests and Cummerbunds

As already stated, formal dressing demands that the waistband of the trousers never be exposed. For this reason, a formal vest or cummerbund is always worn.

The formal vest, though also a descendant of the nineteenth-century English-postboy riding vest, differs considerably from the traditional business vest. It is cut with shawl lapels, either single- or double-breasted, and has a deep **V** front so as to display the special front of the formal shirt. The vest is normally made with three buttons, which can be replaced by studs. The traditional vest is in the same fabric as the dinner jacket.

The pleated cummerbund, which usually matches the facings of the front of the coat, was originally a sash worn in India (from the Hindu *kamarband*) and was brought to the West by the British. The folds of the cummerbund should always point up because, traditionally, the cummerbund had a small pocket between the folds fashioned to hold opera or theater tickets.

The Necktie

The formal tie is, of course, a bow tie. It should never be of the clip-on, pre-tied variety, since, as a practical matter, if one is wearing a wing collar, the clip will be well within view. Aesthetically, a hand-tied bow tie is always more elegant. The color should be black or midnight blue; the style, no larger than the medium-size butterfly (see the illustration on page 126) or the more narrow bat wing shape (see the illustration on page 128); the fabric should always be silk, in a twill, barathea, or satin weave. The texture of the tie should always relate to the facings on the lapels: satin for satin lapels, twill or barathea for grosgrain.

Shoes

Formal wear requires a formal shoe. Again, there are two choices: The patent-leather oxford or the pump. The pump is a low-cut slip-on made of patent or matte-finish leather with a dull ribbed silk bow in front. The oxford is a plain-toe lace-up shoe made with thin soles and a small toe. The more elegant is the pump. While the oxford is clearly the more popular model today, because the pump is considered by many men to be effeminate, it is nevertheless the calf

The patent-leather evening pump.   The patent-leather evening oxford.

pump that is the choice of the more sophisticated dressers. A direct descendant of the opera pump, it can double as a stylish shoe for entertaining at home.

Hosiery

The choice of hose depends upon the color of one's trousers. This means black or dark blue, with shell white or colored clocks, if available. Traditionally, the hose would be of sheer silk. Today semi-sheer lisle, cotton, or fine wool is acceptable.

Jewelry

Simplicity should govern the choice of jewelry for formal wear. Studs and matching cufflinks can be made of plain gold, black enamel, or semi-precious stone. Mother-of-pearl, also handsome, is perhaps more appropriate for white tie. Fine sets of studs and matching cufflinks can be found in antique shops that specialize in old jewelry (the most interesting examples are those made between 1890 and 1930). You might also look for a gold pocket watch and chain. If you choose to wear a wristwatch, remember that the thinner the watch, the more tasteful it is. Black bands are recommended.

Handkerchiefs, Scarves, and Flowers

A properly folded (points showing) white hand-rolled linen handkerchief in the breast pocket is de rigueur. Silk is not quite so elegant because it lacks the body of linen and thus the points go limp when folded. A white or colored silk scarf worn with the outercoat adds yet another touch of style, and a flower provides a dot of color. Never, but never, pin a flower to a lapel. If your jacket does not have a proper buttonhole for a flower, do not wear one.

The Outercoat

It is hardly mandatory in order to be considered well-dressed to have an outercoat specifically designed to be worn with formal or semi-formal wear, but if you decide to make the investment, the single-breasted, fly-front black or dark blue Chesterfield style with velvet collar is the proper complement to the rest of the outfit.

Interesting Options

The greatest modern dressers have always expressed their individuality by bending—though not breaking—the rules. This has been true even in formal wear. If your evening clothes are grounded in the classics, there is no reason you can't add your own particular stamp.

If the whim strikes you, here are some possible interesting options you might try.

For a winter alternative to the tuxedo jacket, there is the single-breasted shawl-collar velvet smoking jacket in garnet, navy, or green. For summer, there is the classic Bogart *Casablanca* white shawl-collar or the colonial tan shawl-collar in silk shantung, both correct in either the single- or double-breasted models. As for bottoms, there are burgundy or white wool trousers.

For a different formal shirt, one might try a pleated front in ivory, blue, pink, or yellow in cotton or silk. The alternative vest choices include black silk, brocade, or a more dressy look in white piqué. For an alternative to the staid black cummerbund, there is solid maroon silk or a fancy brocade.

Like the trousers and vest, the bow tie also lends itself well to expressions of personal creativity. As an accent to the black-and-white motif of the tuxedo, the colors of burgundy, deep red, and purple are the most traditional and most elegant. A small black-and-white pattern is also smart. If you choose a pattern, make certain that the bow tie is woven, not printed, as the latter is not formal enough.

For hosiery, the options are more limited. Choose either burgundy to match the tie or cummerbund, or a medium gray cotton lisle.

As for footwear, monogrammed or motif-embroidered velvet slippers are elegant possibilities.

VIII

Headwear

"Have a good hat; the secret of your looks
Lives with the beaver in Canadian brooks;
Virtue may flourish in an old cravat,
But a man and nature scorn the shocking hat."
—*OLIVER WENDELL HOLMES*

Throughout history what a man has worn on his head has always served to identify either his place or his function in society. Regardless of whether it was an iron helmet worn as protection by a soldier, a crown to denote a king, a coonskin cap to mark the frontiersman and Indian scout, or the high-crowned, wide-brimmed hat of the Pilgrim, each revealed something specific about the wearer.

Besides advertising a man's station in the community, hats have always been considered an integral part of a man's wardrobe. For this reason, up until the mid-twentieth century, no well-dressed gentleman would have dared appear in public without having his head covered.

With the evolution of a more casual society, hats have recently lost a good deal of their former popularity. During the 1960s and '70s, in fact, one would have been hard-pressed to find a man wearing a hat. Perhaps this was due to the popularity of such style-setting non-hat-wearers as John F. Kennedy; perhaps it was simply another mark of the rebellious decade of the sixties; perhaps it was due to the advent of long hairstyles; or perhaps it could be attributed to the narrow-lined, tight-fitting European style of clothing on top of which any hat looked like a sombrero. But whatever the reason, hats faded from the scene for nearly twenty years, and only now are they beginning to re-appear with any frequency.

In America, hatmaking began in the middle to late seventeenth century. During the next one hundred years, this industry grew so rapidly that by 1744, the citizens of New York, New Jersey, and Pennsylvania were all wearing domestically produced hats while, in marked contrast, they were still importing nearly 90 percent of all their other apparel. The American hat industry was so strong, in fact, that the English Parliament was petitioned by a lobby of London felt makers anxious to halt the exportation of hats from the Colonies. "Gad, sir," complained one astonished English hat maker, "it's rebellion when a colony makes better hats than old England!"

As a result, in 1780, the Colonists were forbidden to transport hats from one town to another (of course, this was the kind of legislation that was, like the modern-day "crime" of jaywalking, broken with astounding frequency). By this time, Danbury, Connecticut, had earned the reputation of being the hat center of America. It was here that Zador Benedict, also in 1780, first conceived of the notion of a hat factory. Employing one "journeyman" and two apprentices, Mr. Benedict managed to manufacture eighteen fur hats each week, selling them for between six and ten dollars apiece.

By 1836 sophisticated machinery was beginning to be employed in the manufacture of hats. And it was in 1866 that Rudolph Eickenmeyer and George Osterheld were granted a patent on a hat-blocking and -shaping machine, which went even further in modernizing the hat industry.

Meanwhile, with more hats available to cover more heads, specialty shops began springing up in every major (and many minor) city. It was at this time that many fledgling hat dealers, such as Stetson, Crofut & Knapp, and Dunlap, began to take their place as . the premier hatters in the nation.

By the turn of this century, the type of felt used in modern-day hats had taken form, and by the mid-1930s, all of the basic hat styles that we know today had become staples of the headwear industry.

There are many who believe that a hat is an integral part of a man's wardrobe. While this may be true, it must be added that in this day and age it is no easy matter to wear a hat and look unaffected. Nevertheless, a hat does add immeasurably to a well-dressed look by the style a man chooses and the angle at which he sets it upon his head, both of which provide a reliable clue to his mood and personality.

Those who choose to wear a hat should be careful in making their selections. Not all hats look appropriate on every individual. To begin with, the height of the crown and the width of the brim ought to be in correct proportion to the size and shape of a man's head and face. A man with a narrow face ought to wear a hat with a narrower brim; otherwise, the heavy shadowing of the hat will make his face appear thinner. Conversely, a man with a rounder, wider face, or with facial hair, ought to wear a hat with a wider brim, lest he risk looking like Oliver Hardy.

A good rule to follow when choosing the proper-fitting hat is that its height should be the same as the distance from the middle of the forehead to the top of the crown as the distance from the chin to the middle of the forehead. There is an exception to this, however. Since a hat can add the illusion of height, the shorter man might choose to wear a hat with a slightly higher crown while eschewing those with a shorter crown.

The best hats are made of felt, a material that some mistakenly believe is simply a variety of cloth. It is not. Felt is a fabric that is made of various short, single animal fibers that are interlocked by their natural tendency to "crawl" and twist when water and steam are applied. Felt is the strongest natural material known to man because each fiber is connected in every direction with the adjacent fibers. At the same time, it is light, resilient, and nearly waterproof.

Other qualities of a fine hat include a genuine leather sweatband; a lining that's been sewn in rather than glued; a hand-sewn ribbon on the crown that has been tacked on four sides; and a bow on the hatband. The bow should always be on the left because, traditionally, when a man went into battle, he wore his lady's plume on the left side of his hat not only to show his love but also to keep it out of the way during swordplay.

THE WEARING OF HATS

A hat should never be worn haphazardly. Whether intended or not, it says something very personal about the wearer, and it says it where everyone can see—on the top of his head.

A man chooses the shape of his hat and the way he creases it. He also has a choice in the way he tilts it, for all hats should be worn slightly atilt. With the brim up, he has an open, more approachable look, while wearing it down can make a man appear more mysterious or daring.

In general, soft- or snap-brim hats offer the greatest opportunity for projecting a man's personality. He can direct not only the angle of the tilt but also the shape of the crease and the direction of the brim.

The general rule regarding color is that a hat ought to reflect the color of the topcoat or, if a man is not wearing one, his suit or shoes. However, it is also acceptable to vary the coloration. For example, a gray hat looks smart with a navy coat, especially if the man's suit is gray. Another interesting variation is a green felt hat with a brown tweed coat.

When you put on a hat, always avoid handling it by the crown as this will leave fingerprints on the felt. Grasp it by the front and back of the brim and pull it about halfway down the forehead, then give it the appropriate tilt.

If the hat fits properly, it should hardly be felt on the head. The edges of the hat should barely touch the tops of the ears. (Hat sizes are based upon the diameter of the circumference of one's head. However, one should remember that hats eventually shrink somewhat and thus should never fit snugly when purchased.)

Wearing a hat today takes confidence and a certain élan. If you don't believe you can pull it off, there's no need to feel you must wear one. On the other hand, if you want to add an extra measure of dash to your wardrobe, there is perhaps no better way to do it than with a fine hat.

HAT ETIQUETTE

Hat wearing, with its Old World flavor, carries with it a body of etiquette that should be respected. This is both the pleasure and the responsibility it gives the wearer. It used to be said that there was one sure way of spotting a true gentleman, and that was to observe the first thing he did when he entered a house. If he took off his hat, he was probably a gentleman; if he did not take his hat off, he was only pretending to be a gentleman; if he had no hat on his head in the first place, there was no gentlemanliness about him, in fact or pretense.

For instance, hats should always be removed whenever a man is inside, whether it be in the home, the office, or the lobby of a building. Hats should also be removed in elevators, with the exception, perhaps, of one that is crowded, wherein the wearer runs the risk of getting his chapeau crushed if he correctly places it against his chest. When meeting a woman acquaintance in the street, proper etiquette demands that one's hat should also be tipped in acknowledgment of her presence; this is a holdover of the traditional etiquette of soldiers, who lifted the visors of their helmets to show that they were friendly.

Those not interested in formal ceremony, of course, need not apply.

Hats look best when they have been personalized.

HAT STYLES

For business and elegant casual wear, there are dozens of hat styles from which to choose. But many of these are fashion products of questionable taste and style. If you are inclined to wear a hat, make sure you choose from among the eleven classics that endure not only because of tradition but because of their inherent good style.

The Top Hat

The top hat (or topper) originated in China around 1775, when a Cantonese hatter produced a silk topper to be brought back to France. It is to be worn only for full dress, which means white tie and tails. In the past, the top hat was rigid and made of pure silk plush. Today, however, the top hat is usually an "opera hat" of black grosgrain cloth, stretched over a spring frame, which allows it to be flattened when not in use. This option enables the hat to be slipped under the wearer's seat for safekeeping during a theater performance.

The top hat.

The Homburg

Next to the top hat, the homburg—named for the German spa and resort town of the same name, where it first appeared (and was popularized by King Edward VII)—is the most formal of hats, often favored by ambassadors and members of the foreign service during high state occasions. Proper for day or evening wear, the black or midnight-blue homburg is worn with a dark suit, morning coat in spring or fall, and a Chesterfield coat in winter. This style hat, which looks somewhat better on the older, more mature man, should have a pronounced side curl and a slight dip in the front and back. If one has an oval face, the crown ought not be exceedingly high. The brim, however, should be wider, with a well-defined roll to it.

The homburg.

138

The Fedora

The fedora, named for the Victorien Sardou melodrama of 1882 (*Fédora*, written especially for Sarah Bernhardt), is perhaps the most versatile of hats. It is appropriate for casual day or evening wear. When first introduced, a fedora was a soft felt hat with a crown that was low and tapered and creased lengthwise with a permanently rolled brim. Today, however, most fedoras have a medium-width snap brim (a flexible brim that can be snapped up or adjusted down), with an up to two-inch band around the crown. Narrow-faced men ought to eschew wide-brimmed fedoras, as they only accentuate the thinness of the face.

The fedora.

The Derby

The derby, named for the Earl of Derby who commissioned it, is a dressy, stylish, exclusively daytime hat that gives its wearer a definite British flavor. Also known as the bowler, for its English inventor, or the coke hat, for Bill Coke, the early sponsor of the hat, this style is especially flattering to the man with a narrow face. It is often made of stiff felt, in black, gray, or brown. It is most properly worn with business clothes, topcoats, and overcoats. It is never worn with black tie.

The derby.

The Irish fisherman's hat.

The trilby.

The Trilby

The trilby, or sloucher, named for the heroine of an 1894 George Du Maurier novel, is simply another version of the snap-brim fedora. It is slightly more rigid than the fedora, streamlined, and tapered with a ⅜- to ½-inch band around the crown (usually of grosgrain). Originally associated with a trench coat, it evolved in the 1920s into a soft English country hat with a creased tapered crown worn with a front pinch. Appropriate for informal occasions, the edge of the brim is usually left unfinished, though it may be bound with matching grosgrain. Because of its softness, the trilby can be manipulated into a plethora of shapes. For this reason, the hat has remained popular even during times when most men felt wearing a hat was too conformist a gesture.

The Irish Fisherman's Hat

The soft, crushable Irish fisherman's hat, also known as the Rex Harrison–style hat (after the one he wore in *My Fair Lady*), is a small-brimmed, usually tweedy cloth hat. Appropriate only for casual wear, it is often used to protect its wearer from the elements and is especially popular as a rain hat that can be folded up and kept in one's pocket.

The straw boater (the "sennit").

The Panama optimo.

The Panama and the Straw Boater

These hats are appropriate only for spring and summer wear. The Panama, or optimo-shaped, hat, introduced to this country by sailors returning from that Latin American country just prior to the turn of the century, is lightweight, unlined, and originally came rolled up. Though called the Panama because it was first purchased in that country by sailors and by forty-niners on their way to the California gold fields, it has always been made in the hills of Ecuador. Traditionally, the straw boater, which usually had a two- to three-inch colorful striped or paisley silk band around the crown, was worn only up until Labor Day, after which it was thrown away and a new one purchased the next year.

The Tyrolean Hat

The genuine Tyrolean hat (from the Tyrol region of Austria) was originally made popular in the 1930s, but there was a resurgence of interest in it with the Ivy League look of the 1950s. It has a cord band and plumage and is, once again, only appropriate for casual or sports wear. This is one hat that lends itself particularly to customizing, with its wearer able to dress it up with feathers, pins, and the like. It is appropriately worn with any mixed suit ensemble, sports jackets, polo coats, or trench coats. It should be avoided by men with full faces and is chiefly meant for out-of-doors wear, as in the country or at football games.

The Porkpie

The porkpie, or English pastry hat, received its name from the groove surrounding the flattened top of the crown (hence the English pastry allusion). Normally constructed with a snap brim, they were made for the college market in the mid-1930s and were later popularized by Fred Astaire and Cary Grant. They have long been associated with sporting events, especially horse racing, and therefore are meant for casual wear. This style hat tends to give the wearer a squashed-down appearance and consequently is not particularly flattering to the small man or one with a large face.

The Tyrolean.

The porkpie.

141

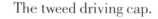

The tweed driving cap.

The Driving Cap

The cloth driving cap became popular around the turn of this century as a replacement for the derby worn for open automobile driving (the derby, of course, had a tendency to be blown off one's head, while the driving cap stayed on more firmly). Its material is usually rough tweed, solid or patterned. It looks best for informal country wear or for attending sporting events.

CARING FOR YOUR HAT

As Fred Astaire once remarked, "I often take a brand-new suit or hat and throw it up against the wall a few times to get that stiff squareness out of it."

Whether one heeds this advice or not, a hat should look as if it's been lived in, while at the same time it ought not look as if it's on the verge of being condemned.

Since a fine hat cleaner is as scarce as the silk top hat today, self-care is a necessity. Using a long-bristled brush, brush your hat each day that you wear it. Due to the nature of felt, with its interlocking fibers, this material tends to collect an abundance of dust. If possible, pass the hat through steam from a kettle while brushing gently in the direction of the nap (against the grain).

If you've been caught out in the rain, it is best to allow a felt hat to dry before brushing it out. If the brim is worn down, turn it up while it dries and it will retain its shape. Do not place it near a radiator or any other excessively hot place, as it is liable to shrink. After it has dried, use a whisk broom to remove spots of mud. A small brush should also be used on cloth or tweed hats. For silk top hats, a velvet pad should be used. If the hat requires blocking, let an expert, such as a fine hat store, do the job.

Hats should always be stored in a separate hatbox. The collapsible opera hat should be stored unfolded in a box with the crown side down. A soft hat must be stored with the crown uncreased and brim up. It must be reshaped each time it is worn. Other kinds of hats—those with permanent creases, such as some fedoras and all homburgs—must be stored in their natural state.

IX
Classic Sportswear

"The man who knows what to avoid
is already the owner of style."
—*W. FOWLER*, *"Matter of Manners"*

Prior to World War I, sportswear was virtually nonexistent in this country. As day-to-day life was far more formal and leisure time at a premium, American men simply did not own separate casual outfits but instead tended to dress for play in much the same way as they did during business hours.

But the end of the war and the new prosperity it provided changed all this. By 1918, the Norfolk jacket, patterned after the Duke of Norfolk's hunting suit, was introduced as what might well be considered the first American sports jacket. It wasn't long before the more affluent man with time on his hands took eagerly to the notion of wearing odd trousers, first with his suit jacket and later with specially designed sports jackets. Not only were these outfits worn as casual country clothes but they were also much in evidence at many of the tonier resorts, such as Palm Beach, Newport, and the French Riviera.

By the mid-1920s, knickers began to appear on the sportswear fashion scene and were especially visible on the golf links. And when the Prince of Wales was seen wearing knickers while touring South American cattle ranches, their popularity was assured. Also during this period when men were experimenting with leisure wear, various styles of trousers meant to be worn for casual occasions were introduced. Among these were white and striped flannels and the Oxford bags, which had been worn by Cambridge and Oxford students over their knickers when these garments were banned from the classrooms.

By the middle of the 1930s, however, knickers had all but vanished from a man's sports wardrobe as they were replaced by odd trousers of lightweight materials such as linen, cotton, poplin, and lightweight woolen and worsted fabrics. Although these trousers were available in a wide variety of stripes, patterns, and solid colors, it was dark gray—and in the summer or at winter resorts, white—that was the most popular. Flannel trousers were also high on the list, as the accepted resort "uniform" was a navy blue polo shirt and gray flannel slacks.

In the matter of sports shirts, only polo contributed a special shirt to be worn for leisure activities. This short-sleeved wool jersey pullover with a turned-down collar was first introduced in this country by Brooks Brothers around the turn of the century and has remained popular ever since. Those who preferred tennis or golf were forced to wear a soft voilelike shirt with the sleeves rolled up. It wasn't until 1928, when a knitted cotton tennis shirt first appeared on the French Riviera (where many of the sportswear fashions originated) that other sportsmen had a shirt they could wear while participating in leisure activities. Like a polo shirt, this short-sleeve shirt had a turned-down collar, and opened in front about five inches from the top button. It was only a matter of months before this sports shirt crossed the Atlantic and became a favorite at Palm Beach.

It was in the decade of the 1930s, however, that the sportswear industry in this country truly exploded. By this time, the wealthier man was particularly concerned about how he looked away from the office; thus he experimented widely with what was called semi-sportswear. While still wearing a tie, he donned a variety of sport-styled jackets as well as finely patterned sports shirts (both long- and short-sleeve), odd trousers, and sweaters. This newfound interest in sportswear even crossed over into the business sector as men, returning from the country, slowly integrated their "country gentleman" wardrobe into their business attire. This included tweed raglan-shouldered topcoats, sleeveless sweaters and cardigans in place of proper vests, and tattersall soft-collared shirts. The 1932 Winter Olympics in Lake Placid, New York, also contributed to the sportswear boom, as skiing and hence ski clothes gained in popularity.

With the 1940s came the California influence on sportswear. Trousers with short belt loops and narrow belts replaced the beltless wide-waistband trousers of the thirties, and in came new colors for menswear, such as blue-green, gold, bright yellow, and russet. This love affair with color was also reflected in the sports shirts of the period. In fact, it was during the forties that the Hawaiian shirt first made it to the mainland and enjoyed a brief but widespread popularity. Thirty years later it once again garnered a new body of loyalists.

Even the staid 1950s saw sportswear remain on the flamboyant side, as men who were partial to gray flannel suits during the workweek often spent their weekends at the country club or in the countryside wearing loud plaid jackets and madras trousers or Bermuda shorts.

This set the stage for the 1960s, when, in line with other aspects of the menswear industry, sportswear went overboard, offering all kinds of highly stylized, even bizarre, fashions in colors that came from the widest ends of the spectrum. But perhaps the greatest change that took place in dressing during this decade was the enormous popularity and acceptance of jeans for casual wear. This jeans explosion, first involving the traditional Levi's and Wranglers and then leading to the production of "designer" jeans, very much changed the way Americans dressed during their leisure time. Now men began to think differently about what it meant to wear clothes to relax in, as jeans gave them an option they'd never had before.

The 1970s was the era of the designer in sportswear. Every designer who entered the menswear industry and wanted to make a statement about fashion did it with sportswear. It was a period of great excitement, and it piqued interest in the style of clothing men wore for the first time in many years. Consequently, new sportswear was introduced each season, often contradicting styles of the previous season. There were updated athletic clothes designed to be worn out of the gym, disco wear became common on the street, and T-shirts with designer logos abounded.

Today, in the eighties, Americans seem to be returning to the more traditional kinds of sportswear. Though athletic wear is still quite popular, some of the extremes in sportswear have been eliminated. For the very young, there are still avant-garde fashions, but designers are no longer trying to force the mature man into a highly stylized uniform. Shetland sweaters, corduroy trousers, and button-down-collar shirts are back, but they are worn now with a new contemporary flavor.

In the last ten years, no segment of the menswear industry has shown as much growth as that of sportswear. But this tremendous growth, offering a myriad of possibilities to the American man, has also offered the greatest potential for lapses in taste.

To the American clothing industry, the manufacture of sportswear most often involves the packaging of specific "outfits" and matched "separates" designed to be worn in a given way. This concept tends to discourage any sense of individuality. The stylish dresser generally resists such programmatic attire for his leisure time. Instead, he puts together whatever he happens to have around—a sports jacket that might have been worn to work, say, with an open-neck shirt, tossing on a silk foulard neckerchief, a sweater with an odd pair of trousers. This requires more thought and imagination than the conventional department-store approach, which would be simply to don a matched outfit. But the style achieved by the well-dressed man will be more individual, and in the long run it will be more economical as well. Classic separates of sportswear will not go out of style the way a matched outfit will.

This is not to say that one should never buy specific sportswear items for use during leisure hours. But one should be aware that the sportswear sector has always been the most fashion-conscious part of the menswear industry. Its designs change rapidly from season to season in order to bolster sales. Thus it is the area with the greatest degree of built-in obsolescence.

Because sportswear is so varied and so personal, it is difficult to circumscribe it with a body of unbending rules. However, there are some general principles that must, as a minimum, be followed to ensure a look of style and sophistication.

To begin with, there is absolutely no excuse for buying matched ensembles. Because of the casual nature of sportswear, it should have a less studied look, and these kinds of outfits always end up looking contrived. Indeed, the more highly styled the leisure outfit, the quicker one is likely to become bored with it. Instead, match things casually. Sportswear should look as if it is your own, not someone else's.

Avoid styles that exaggerate particular details, such as excess padding, oversized collars, extra buttons, zippers and snaps, and pockets that serve no purpose. In short, details should be functional. The garment should not be over-designed (and this applies to pattern as well). There is no point, for instance, in having elbow patches on a new sports jacket.

Designer initials or logos should be avoided. Someone else's initials do not belong on your clothing, especially if the goal of wearing clothing is to make it your own, to project your own sense of individuality. As the classic *New Yorker* cartoon character remarked when a salesman tried to sell him a shirt with the YSL monogram on it, "If I was meant to have that shirt, my mother would have named me Yves Saint-Laurent." Often it is impossible to avoid buying a shirt without a designer's logo, primarily because of marketing pressure from department stores. However, if you are forced to wear an item that has a designer's logo on it, make sure the logo is simple and unobtrusive.

Sportswear should be made only of natural materials. Why should the clothes one wears for relaxation provide any less comfort and style than those worn for business? But there is a functional reason that goes beyond the aesthetic. When wearing sports clothing, a man, rather than remaining sedentary, is most likely to be moving around a good deal. Natural fibers breathe, thus allowing improved air circulation, which helps cool the body. At the same time, natural fibers absorb perspiration.

Generally, sportswear ought to be looser-fitting than business wear. Not only does this allow for the increased movement of the body, but it permits a man to layer his outfit, adding an extra shirt or sweater when necessary. Shirts and sports jackets, for instance, may be cut a bit fuller in the body. And yet there is no reason sportswear should not follow the basic lines of the body. There should be no sacrifice of comfort for design.

Americans have always had a strong predilection for color. Their bodies are large, and they carry reds, greens, deep yellow, and blues without feeling those colors reflect negatively on their masculinity. Casual occasions are a fine opportunity to wear colors that are proscribed from a serious business environment.

Today more and more people are wearing athletic wear in their leisure time. Unfortunately, this has been taken to the extreme. Athletic wear should be reserved for the activity for which it was made. Nothing looks sillier than attending a professional tennis match wearing a matched tennis outfit—except perhaps wearing a sweatsuit out to dine.

The following presentation contains items of sport clothing that have been manufactured in a similar style for at least the past thirty years and have achieved the status of classics. While they may go in and out of the moment's "fashion" during the next decade, they will never go out of style. For this reason, one need not spend much time worrying over how to coordinate them. The great appeal of sportswear is its unpredictability. If you use classics, even the most ill-coordinated combination will not push you beyond the bounds of good taste.

FALL/WINTER SPORTSWEAR

Crocodile belt.

Cotton knit turtleneck.

Calf tassel Loafers.

Shetland multicolor-striped hand-knitted sweater.

Cashmere and silk neckerchief.

Wool or cotton striped knitted long-sleeve polo shirt.

The Levi's 501 tapered-leg jeans.

148

Hand-framed block-pattern crewneck.

Printed cotton-wool flannel country shirt.

Silk muffler for wearing with an outercoat.

Reverse calf suede oxfords.

Hand-knitted Peruvian alpaca sweater.

Pleated gray flannels.

Sleeveless hand-knitted Fair Isle pullover.

1950s rayon garbardine second-hand H. Bar C. cowboy shirt.

English storm-proof shooting jacket of oiled cotton.

Wool bird's-eye-type socks.

Tartan plaid trousers.

Cashmere cardigan.

Suede hip-length weekend jacket.

150

Shetland country walking socks.

Knitted English wool-rib waistcoat.

Cowboy boots.

Argyle pattern wool hose.

Cotton sweat pants.

Viyella cotton-wool plaid sportshirt.

Knitted wool cable-stitch sweater.

Striped cotton duck trousers.

Cotton rib crewneck.

Cotton argyle hose.

Cotton madras button-down.

Cotton sport trunks.

Wool hand-loomed cable tennis pullover.

Striped cotton lisle shirt.

Cotton boat-neck sweater.

Cotton ten-month drizzler jacket.

Cotton argyle pullover.

Printed corduroy slacks.

Navy canvas boat sneaker.

Cotton Fair Isle sleeveless cardigan.

Cotton safari jacket.

Madras swim trunks or shorts.

Top-Siders.

Cotton short-sleeve shirt.

Summer belts.

Irish linen plaid neckerchief.

Cotton bird's-eye pattern socks.

The Brooks Brothers fun shirt.

Cotton fun-print pants.

Hand-knitted cotton summer pullover.

1950s rayon gabardine Hawaiian shirt.

Espadrilles.

Sea Island cotton lisle polo shirt.

Cotton polo shirt.

White bucks.

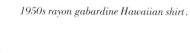

100 percent cotton khakis.

155

X
The Wardrobe: Fall/Winter and Spring/Summer

"Take great care always to be dressed like the
reasonable people of your own age, in the place
where you are; whose dress is never spoken of
one way or another as either too negligent or
too much studied."

—*LORD CHESTERFIELD, in a letter to his son*

What do the world's fine dressers all have in common? It is not
that they dress in a similar fashion. Cary Grant's wardrobe, for
instance, is certainly not the one favored by Fred Astaire. Yet both
these men have always been considered among the elite dressers of
the twentieth century. In fact, there is something about their dress
that sets them apart from the majority of men. The secret—if it is a
secret at all—is that each item of clothing worn by these and other
fine dressers is of consummate taste and quality. At the same time,
these men have always looked completely at home in their clothes,
as if the clothes were theirs and theirs alone.

Wearing clothes of quality requires that one use only those
items made of the finest materials, those whose design adheres to
the traditions of classic tailoring. Only these items can help the
wearer avoid the pitfalls of changing fashion. If a man fills his
wardrobe with such apparel, he virtually cannot go wrong in the
way he dresses. Whatever he puts together will look well—some
combinations better than others. Yet even the worst mismatching
will never be a catastrophe; more likely, it will be viewed as an
interesting personal—one might even say idiosyncratic—gesture.

Beginning in the 1930s, men realized that to look truly elegant, their clothes had to be subtle. Only the arriviste wore anything obvious. As Beau Brummell, the famous nineteenth-century dandy who personified the ultimate in understated elegance, once observed, "If a person turns to observe your dress, you are not well-dressed; instead, your clothes are either too new, too tight, or too fashionable."

Recognizing quality and fine classic styling in the clothes you wear has been the subject of preceding chapters. Putting these clothes together in an acceptable personal style is the goal here. The development of a personal style begins with taking an objective view of your own physical characteristics: Are you short or tall, heavy or thin? What is your skin coloring? Having this knowledge allows you to minimize any peculiarities and to wear clothes that flatter rather than detract from your appearance. The following paragraphs contain recommendations for those who need to take special care in their dressing. They are general suggestions, not rules that can't be bent. If there is a choice between a stylish suit and one that merely follows a specific guideline, opt for the stylish suit. You may not look as thin or as tall or as narrow, but these are only minor objectives within the greater goal of dressing well.

THE HEAVY MAN

For the heavier man, the basic goal in dressing is to accentuate the vertical lines of the body. Avoid blatant colors and bold patterns. In large quantity, color is an eye attracter and can make a heavy man look like a walking billboard. Chalk-stripe and herringbone patterns are recommended because of their vertical lines. Plaids are fine, but the vertical warp ought to be more pronounced than the horizontal woof. Smooth fabrics, such as sharkskins and worsteds, should be used. Avoid bulky tweeds and wear clothes of saxonies and cheviots instead.

Clothes should be cut generously; nothing stresses bulges more than skimpy clothing. The jacket should be slightly longer than normal and hang straight down in back. Sleeves should be tapered and trouser bottoms somewhat narrower than usual. Double-breasted jackets that button on the bottom button are recommended because of the elongating effect this line gives the lapel. Trousers with pleats so that the pockets are easily accessible should be worn on the waistline. Shirt collars should not be rounded, and the collar points ought to lead away from the front of the face.

Topcoats should be shorter, hemmed just to the bottom of the knee, thus lengthening the distance to the ground. Shoes should be kept simple, without a lot of toe decoration. Hat crowns should always taper, and the brim should be of medium width.

THE SHORT MAN

The primary goal of the short man is the same as that of the heavy man. The short man looks to elongate his line, so he and the heavy man should favor the same fabrics and patterns. However, the shoulders of the short man's jacket can be more squared, thereby raising the eye farther from the floor. Jacket length is critical. If a jacket is too short, it will cut the short man's body in half; if it is too long, it will make his legs appear to be shorter than they are. Trousers should be tapered at the bottom a bit more than normal. Avoid dainty shoes in favor of bluchers, monk straps, or reverse calves. It is often recommended that shorter men avoid cuffs on their trousers, but the little that is gained in the illusion of height is invariably lost in style. Besides, cuffs are more consistent in relationship to the heavier shoe. Topcoats should be knee-length with the lapels long-rolled. Hats should have a tall, sloping crown, and the brim can be wide.

THE TALL MAN

The requirements of the tall man are diametrically opposed to those of the heavy or short man. Here it is the horizontal line that is to be accentuated, in order to stress breadth. Patterns that accomplish this are diagonals and overplaids. Fabrics should be unfinished worsteds, tweeds, and other bulky materials. Clothing should be fitted generously, jackets tailored on the long side with a loose waist and an extra bit of width in the shoulders. Double-breasted jackets are good in that they tend to have wider lapels than single-breasted models. When buttoned at the waist, they add to the illusion of heft. Trousers should always be cuffed.

The most flattering outercoats for the tall man are double-breasted with long lapels. They should be worn below the knee. Hats should have a low crown and a moderate brim size.

SKIN AND HAIR COLOR

Finely styled, classic business clothes are manufactured in traditional mainstream colors that have continued to flatter most men over the past fifty years. There are, however, a few men who have special coloring conditions and, as a result, must be somewhat more circumspect in choosing from among these suits. These are redheads, fair-haired and light-skinned men, and those older men with gray or white hair. Fortunately, the limitations are few.

Redheads ought to avoid brilliant colors, especially reds. Warm browns, medium grays, and gray-greens look best. Fair-haired men have a somewhat wider selection in the range of colors, but they should avoid light shades of gray, tan, and yellow. These will tend to make them look sallow. Finally, those men with gray or white hair should avoid pale tones unless they prefer to look completely inconspicuous when they enter a room.

GETTING DRESSED

When putting an outfit together, the fine dresser recognizes that there are four elements that need to be related. These are the suit jacket, the shirt, the tie, and the handkerchief. (The super-sophisticated dresser will often bring a fifth element into play— the hose.) These items can be related in one of two ways: by tonal harmony or by tonal contrast. Tonal harmony is achieved by combining different shades of a single color. It is the simpler of the two possibilities, the safer and perhaps the less interesting as well. An example of this would be a man wearing a pale blue shirt, dark blue tie, and dark blue socks with a navy suit. Certainly this presentation, which was favored by no less than Cary Grant on occasion (the most famous instance perhaps was the outfit he wore in Alfred Hitchcock's *North by Northwest*), cannot be faulted, but it does have a certain predictability. After all, how many times can a man eat steak?

On the other hand, tonal contrast, or the wearing of accessories in colors different from that of the suit, offers unlimited possibilities. Instead of wearing a blue shirt with a navy suit, one might wear a yellow shirt, a tie of burgundy or gray, a handkerchief of soft yellow, and hose of burgundy or gray. If you matched a medium gray end-on-end shirt with a navy chalk-stripe suit, you could wear a tie with navy stripes that had almost any color ground. If the ground was burgundy, you could pick up that color in either the hose or, more obviously, in the handkerchief, such as in a white handkerchief with a burgundy trim. If the ground was gold, you would not want to put gold in your hose, but you could sport a patterned handkerchief that had gold figures. Obviously, dressing in tonal contrast requires considerable attention to detail and sophistication on the part of the wearer. But the rewards are definitely worth the extra effort.

Whether one is putting the day's outfit together employing tonal harmony or tonal contrast, the mixing of patterns that are not compatible can ruin the effect of an otherwise well-coordinated ensemble. The following are some guidelines regarding the mixing of patterns.

1. Avoid wearing patterns that are similar to one another. A bird's-eye suit, for instance, should not be worn with a small-check shirt. Likewise, a mini-check shirt should not be paired with a small-pattern tie. A pin-striped suit should be worn with a hairline-striped shirt rather than one with moderately wide stripes. Thus, stripes of varying gauges may be used.

2. Small, neat patterns should be used to contrast with large, bolder patterns. A striped shirt can be worn with a neat-pattern tie as long as the scale of each pattern differs.

3. Avoid overdoing any one pattern, such as ensembles consisting of all plaids or all stripes. Contrast within one basic type of pattern is acceptable, even desirable. A plaid suit can be combined with a diminutive-check shirt as long as there is the equalizer of a solid tie.

4. Vary the textures of your accessories. If you are wearing a silk tie, a linen handkerchief is preferable to a silk one. If you are wearing a drier fabric tie, such as a wool challis or linen, balance it with the sheen of a silk handkerchief.

5.   Besides clothing the chest, the purpose of the dress shirt is to break up the monotony of the suit. In winter, shirt colors should be light to contrast with dark wool suits; in summer, light-color gabardines and linens should be paired with more deeply hued shirtings.

THE WARDROBE

The businessman needs a wardrobe that offers him acceptability, versatility, and style. The following are the traditional building blocks for a wardrobe that meets those criteria.

The Winter Suits and Jackets
1.   Dark gray worsted
2.   Solid navy
3.   Three-piece gray flannel
4.   Double-breasted chalk-stripe in navy or gray
5.   Muted glenurquhart plaid
6.   Tweed herringbone
7.   Single- or double-breasted blue blazer
8.   Patterned sports jacket—herringbone, gun check, glen plaid

The Spring Suits and Jackets
1.   Dark gray tropical worsted
2.   Gray or navy nine-month three-piece pin-stripe (vest to be removed in summer)
3.   Summer-weight glen plaid
4.   Tan gabardine or tropical wool worsted
5.   Cotton poplin in olive or beige
6.   Blue-and-white or gray-and-white seersucker
7.   Single- or double-breasted lightweight blue blazer
8.   Patterned sports jacket—plaid madras, seersucker, linen, or silk blend

Only the first two suits for winter and summer would be mandatory for every businessman's wardrobe. After these, the order would vary according to individual tastes and needs. However, if your personal economics makes it impossible for you to buy more than one winter suit, the gray worsted would probably be preferable for a man under thirty, since a solid navy suit may look overly austere for a young person.

Shirts

The following list is based on the theory that a man wears one shirt a day and needs an ample stock since his soiled shirts will probably be at the laundry for a week. There are fewer summer shirts, since it is assumed that a number of the winter shirts can be worn all year round.

The Winter Shirts

1. Two white
2. Three blue: one broadcloth, two end-on-end
3. Two other solid colors: yellow or pink in oxford, pinpoint oxford, or end-on-end
4. Six striped: four with self-collar, two with contrast collar
5. Two tattersall
6. One muted plaid

The Summer Shirts

1. Two open-weave shirts: voile, batiste, or basket-weave
2. Two to three solid in pastel shades: pink, maize, purple, peach in pinpoint oxford, broadcloth, or end-on-end
3. Three striped in brighter pastel colors
4. Two brighter-color patterned shirts: candy stripes or windowpane

Ties

The following ties coordinate with the traditional man's wardrobe. There should be approximately twenty-five ties from which to choose. Fall ties are generally darker, the patterns woven instead of printed. For spring, the ties are lighter in color and bolder in design, with spring prints providing a splash of color to the summer business suit.

1. Four solids in twill or grenadine: navy, burgundy, maize, and black
2. Six repp
3. Four small-figured woven silk
4. Two club
5. Five printed silk: two English madder for fall; three foulards of varying sizes and scales for spring
6. Two wool challis
7. One linen solid and one plaid

Pages 163–86 present photographs and descriptions of both fall/winter and spring/winter wardrobes. They represent my personal taste and should not be viewed as outfits to be copied directly.

A

1. The dark gray worsted: the one business suit
every man should own.

A. *suit:* J. Press, Inc.
   shirt: Brooks Brothers
   tie: Alan Flusser
   handkerchief:
   Brooks Brothers

B. *shirt:* Paul Stuart
   tie: Polo by Ralph Lauren
   handkerchief:
   Brooks Brothers

B

2. The navy suit: a must for any well-dressed businessman.

A. *suit:* Sills of Cambridge
    shirt: F. R. Tripler & Co.
    tie: Dunhill Tailors
    handkerchief:
    Brooks Brothers

B. *shirt:* H. Herzfeld
    tie: Alan Flusser
    handkerchief:
    Brooks Brothers

3. The gray flannel: a symbol of America in the 1950s.

A. *suit:* Alan Flusser
   shirt: Brooks Brothers
   tie: Brooks Brothers
   handkerchief: Chipp, Inc.

B. *shirt:* Alan Flusser
   tie: Bergdorf Goodman
   handkerchief:
      Paul Stuart

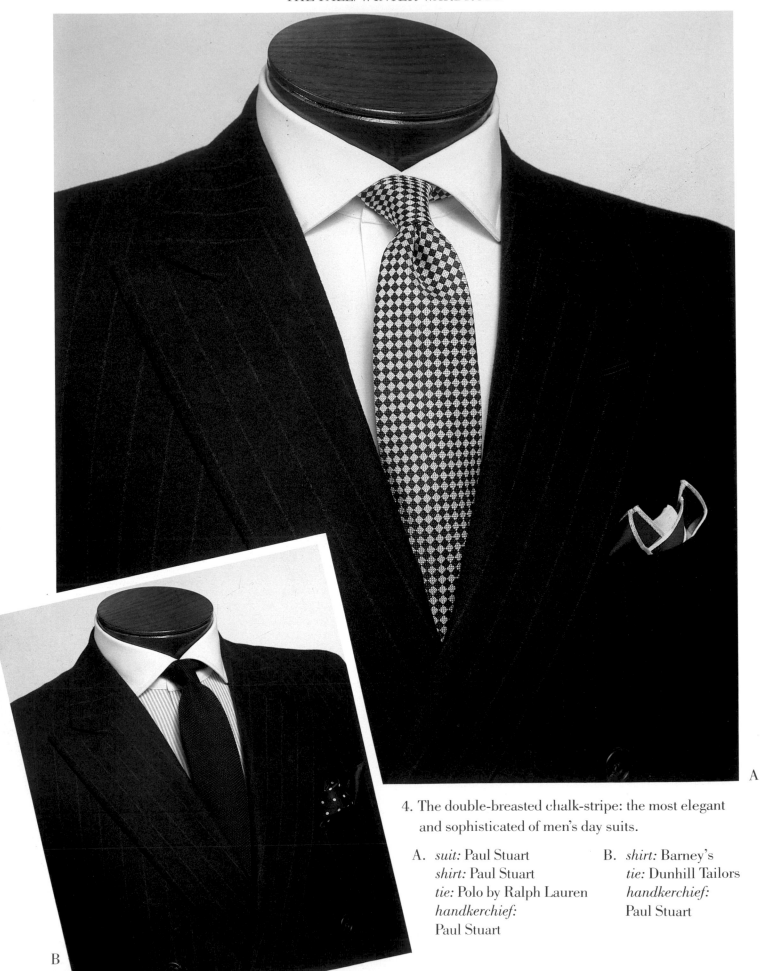

4. The double-breasted chalk-stripe: the most elegant
   and sophisticated of men's day suits.

A. *suit:* Paul Stuart
   shirt: Paul Stuart
   tie: Polo by Ralph Lauren
   handkerchief:
   Paul Stuart

B. *shirt:* Barney's
   tie: Dunhill Tailors
   handkerchief:
   Paul Stuart

5. The muted glenurquhart: the consummate business suit.

A. *suit:* Paul Stuart
    shirt: J. Press, Inc.
    tie: Paul Stuart
    handkerchief:
    Brooks Brothers

B. *shirt:* Paul Stuart
    tie: Brooks Brothers
    handkerchief:
    Brooks Brothers

6. The tweed herringbone: a business suit with a country flavor.

A. *suit:* Paul Stuart
    shirt: Brooks Brothers
    tie: H. Herzfeld
    handkerchief: Alan Flusser

B. *shirt:* Brooks Brothers
    tie: Polo by Ralph Lauren
    handkerchief: Paul Stuart

A

7. The blue blazer: there is no substitute for it.

A. *jacket:* Alan Flusser
   shirt: Paul Stuart
   tie: Brooks Brothers
   handkerchief:
   Alan Flusser

B. *shirt:* Chipp, Inc.
   tie: J. Press, Inc.
   handkerchief:
   Paul Stuart

B

8. The patterned sports jacket: the kind of sartorial friend
   one wants around for a long time.

A. *jacket:* J. Press, Inc.   B. *shirt:* Brooks Brothers
   shirt: Chipp, Inc.   *tie:* Polo by Ralph Lauren
   tie: Polo by Ralph Lauren   *vest:* H. Herzfeld
   handkerchief: *handkerchief:*
   Paul Stuart   Paul Stuart

1. The dark gray tropical worsted: the most important business suit for summer.

A. *suit:* Polo by Ralph Lauren
    shirt: Brooks Brothers
    tie: H. Herzfeld
    handkerchief:
    Brooks Brothers

B. *shirt:* F. R. Tripler & Co.
    tie: Polo by Ralph Lauren
    handkerchief:
    Brooks Brothers

2. The classic gray pin-stripe: in eleven-ounce wool, this three-piece classic can be worn nine months of the year.

A. *suit:* Brooks Brothers
   shirt: H. Herzfeld
   tie: Polo by Ralph Lauren
   handkerchief:
   Brooks Brothers

B. *shirt:* Sills of Cambridge
   tie: Barney's
   handkerchief:
   Alan Flusser

A

3. The glen plaid: the suiting most identified with
the Duke of Windsor.

A. *suit:* Dunhill Tailors
shirt: Alan Flusser
tie: Paul Stuart
handkerchief:
Brooks Brothers

B. *shirt:* Dunhill Tailors
tie: Paul Stuart
handkerchief:
Brooks Brothers

B

4. The tan gabardine: summer's most luxurious suit.

A. *suit:* Alan Flusser
   shirt: Paul Stuart
   tie: Chipp, Inc.
   handkerchief:
   Paul Stuart

B. *shirt:* Brooks Brothers
   tie: Polo by Ralph Lauren
   handkerchief:
   Brooks Brothers

5. The cotton poplin: the perfect knockabout suit
   for the active businessman.

A. *suit:* Brooks Brothers   B. *shirt:* Brooks Brothers
   shirt: Paul Stuart   *tie:* Chipp, Inc.
   tie: Chipp, Inc.   *handkerchief:*
   handkerchief: Paul Stuart
   Paul Stuart

6. The oxford-striped seersucker:
the all-American summer suit.

A. *suit:* Alan Flusser
shirt: Brooks Brothers
tie: Brooks Brothers
handkerchief:
Brooks Brothers

B. *shirt:* Brooks Brothers
tie: Chipp, Inc.
handkerchief:
Brooks Brothers

A.

7. The summer blazer: the perfect foil for summer's bold shirtings
   and bright accessories.

A. *jacket:* Dunhill Tailors
   shirt: Dunhill Tailors
   tie: Chipp, Inc.
   handkerchief:
   Paul Stuart

B. *shirt:* Brooks Brothers
   tie: Polo by Ralph Lauren
   handkerchief:
   Paul Stuart

B

8. The summer sports jacket: a country club classic that is as American as the white buck shoe.

A. *jacket:* Alan Flusser
    shirt: Brooks Brothers
    tie: Polo by Ralph Lauren
    handkerchief:
    Paul Stuart

B. *shirt:* Brooks Brothers
    tie: Alan Flusser
    handkerchief:
    Paul Stuart

THE FALL/WINTER WARDROBE

1. The Dark Gray Worsted

If a man were to own only one business suit, this would be it. The dark gray worsted offers formality, assurance, and versatility. The particular suit shown is an English version made in a sharkskin weave. The added texture gives it a richer feel than a plain all-gray worsted. The white broadcloth straight-point-collar shirt is crisp and clean. It is paired with a burgundy four-in-hand, this country's number-one best-selling color. The club pattern is woven onto the textured burgundy ground, not printed. The white Irish-linen handkerchief with hand-rolled edges is a no-nonsense complement. Its straight points echo the straight points of the collar.

Variation: The versatility of this suit allows a plethora of options. Almost any solid-color shirt would be suitable. For a little bit more visual interest, a blue-and-white-striped end-on-end broadcloth shirt has been substituted for the stark white. The collar remains the same to maintain the formality of the look. Paired with this is a woven neat-pattern red-ground tie. The hue accent of the tie complements the blue striping of the shirt. The patterned tie and shirt do not fight each other because of the different size of their respective patterns.

2. The Navy Suit

Along with the gray worsted, the navy suit is a must for any well-dressed businessman. Its attributes are its formality, the aura of authority it projects, and the richness of color it adds to most men's complexions. However, it may look a little overpowering on a young man. To soften its formality, a medium blue broadcloth shirt with straight-point collar is worn instead of the obvious white. The tie has a navy ground, and the three shades of blue work to create a tonal harmony.

Variation: The traditional blue business suit has left the bank for an elegant evening at the Rainbow Room. The shirt is that most dramatic legacy of the Duke of Windsor: a white cutaway collar contrasting with a blue end-on-end body. The polka-dot tie is simplicity itself. The polka-dot pattern—the most ancient to be put on a necktie—has been woven into the tie, not printed on it. The dots are white, since it is always better to have white in the tie when wearing a shirt with a contrasting white collar; ditto for the handkerchief.

3. The Gray Flannel

The gray flannel suit was a symbol of America in the 1950s. No longer the province of the conservative businessman, this suit is sophisticated and urbane. It is slightly less dressy than the blue or gray worsted suit and somewhat more limited in its wearability. The weight of its cloth makes it a purely winter suit. The gray flannel vest is traditional. The rougher texture of the cloth demands a rougher-finish shirt; this striped oxford button-down shirt gives the suit a collegiate flavor. The striping on the navy tie is widely enough spaced to contrast with the thick striping of the oxford shirt. The colors of the handkerchief reflect the colors of the shirt and tie. Printed silk handkerchiefs always look best in the puff fold, as this shows the center pattern of the handkerchief while hiding its machine-turned edges.

Variations: The tab collar gives an aura of formality. In the example shown, it is somewhat countrified by the tattersall pattern, a direct reference to the flannel's English origins. The figured wool challis tie with its matte finish is a perfect mate for the dull luster of the flannel. The navy silk handkerchief adds a needed vibrancy to the dryness of the tie-suit combination, pairing up well with the sheen of the broadcloth shirt.

4. The Double-Breasted Chalk-Stripe

Perhaps the most elegant and sophisticated of men's day suits, the double-breasted chalk-stripe has few peers. The purchase of this suit is a commitment to style. The white cutaway-collar shirt, of a fine, long-staple pima cotton, is refined and only slightly less dressy than a formal evening shirt. The macclesfield pattern of the tie anchors this outfit clearly in the English tradition. Unlike in England, where striped suits are commonplace, an American will not go unnoticed in the boardroom. An additional natty touch: the blue trim on the white handkerchief.

Variation: The key to the combination of these stripings is the difference in scale. The white cutaway collar has been chosen again because its wide angle corresponds to the crisscrossing of the double-breasted lapels. The maroon grenadine tie is plain, yet the material has enough surface interest to attract the eye. The presence of the solid tie gives one the liberty to wear a patterned handkerchief.

5. The Muted Glenurquhart Plaid

This is the consummate business suit, a muted glen plaid with a
blue windowpane pattern; lively in pattern and yet acceptable in any
working environment. The solid blue shirt brings out the accent
color of the suit. The rounded-pin collar is for those who enjoy a
little more precision in their dress. The silver pin is preferred to
gold here because of the general coloration of the ensemble. The
paisley pattern of this tie is of the right scale to accommodate
the plaid patterning of the suit. The subtle colors of the tie
tastefully blend with the muted colors of the suit.

Variation: There is nothing more pleasing to a clothing
fancier than to be able to meld pattern upon pattern. In this
example, the simplicity of the tie's striping allows it to be combined
with the striped shirt and plaid suit. The three patterns might be too
constricting were it not for the mutedness of the glen-plaid suit. In
the distance, the material could almost be mistaken for a solid. The
combination of the three patterns dictate the choice of a solid
handkerchief.

6. The Tweed Herringbone

The tweed suit has a rural heritage, but with a smart striped tie it
becomes suitable for business wear. The roughness of the fabric (a
winter-weight herringbone) demands either texture or color in the
accessories. The tattersall shirt gives the outfit color and life, and
the striped tie creates a slightly more serious look. The beige linen
handkerchief with gray edge is subtle, less harsh than a white
handkerchief would be, and supports the tonal quality of the outfit.

Variation: This is the ultimate professorial get-up, Ivy League
to the bone; repp-striped bow tie, oxford button-down shirt, and
tweed suit. One sartorial surprise: the forest-green handkerchief
with contrasting brown border.

7. The Blue Blazer

As an odd jacket, there is no substitute for a blue blazer. This
double-breasted model of medium-weight woolen flannel, made with
open patch pockets and polished brass buttons, is an exact copy of
the original worn on the nineteenth-century English frigate the

H.M.S. *Blazer.* The blazer offers tremendous adaptability. Certainly proper for social gatherings and occasionally even appropriate for business, its rich blue color lends itself to a myriad of potential color, pattern, and textural combinations. It is the perfect mate for that class men's trouser, the gray flannel, though it looks equally well with charcoal flannel, dun-colored cavalry twills, or brightly colored corduroys. There is no shirt color or fabric inappropriate for the blazer. In this instance, a blue-and-white candy-striped shirt with a straight-point pin collar has been coupled with a red wool challis print tie. The yellow color in the tie enhances the luster of the blazer's brass buttons and is reflected also in the jacket, shirt, and tie without competing with the scale of the pattern of the shirt and tie.

Variation: Unwilling to ignore such a propitious opportunity for patterning, the blazer has now been mated with an oxford-stripe club-collared shirt, striped figured tie, and silk foulard handkerchief. Yellow is once again the accent color to heighten the interest of the buttons. The oxford cloth of the shirt and silk repp of the tie are historic fabrics that clearly wed the blazer to the classic tradition.

8. The Patterned Sports Jacket

The Shetland glen-plaid sports jacket, colorful and warm, is the kind of sartorial friend one wants around for a long time. As an item of leisure, it demands comparable accessories. The rich texture of the oxford cloth shirt is a fitting partner to the nubby weave of the jacket. The tie is a silk madder paisley print, its muted tone in keeping with the tone set by the jacket. The silk foulard handkerchief brings out the colors of the jacket and tie—a luminous note in an otherwise muted still-life.

Variation: Vests or V-neck sweaters look especially smart with a bow tie, not only covering the space beneath it but framing the tie and shirt collar, thus focusing the presentation. The shirt collar and figures of the tie are intended to enhance the accent colors of the sports jacket. The red ground of the silk handkerchief is in the same family as the pink tone of the oxford shirt; the green and blue figures relate to the green in the tie and the blue in the jacket.

THE SPRING/SUMMER WARDROBE

1. The Dark Gray Tropical Worsted

The charcoal gray tropical worsted is the summer equivalent of the gray winter worsted. Again, if a man had only one business suit for summer, this would be it. Made in a nine-ounce wool fabric, it is light and cool, yet there is no compromise in the high level of formality it creates. Spring and summer allow the wearer to be a bit more adventurous in the choice of accessories. The contrasting white pin-collar shirt was an innovation of a small group of natty stockbrokers in the 1920s. The white collar adds a fitting brightness for summer. The pattern of the tie is printed, not woven, for a lighter effect, and thus is more appropriate for summer. The white accent color in the tie offers a response to the white color of the collar and handkerchief.

Variation: The easiest way to give spring life to a business suit is to pair it with a yellow ground tie. The shirt shown is a burgundy-and-white pin-stripe—a perfect setting for this English print silk tie. The collar is straight-point, simple but elegant.

2. The Classic Gray Pin-Stripe

This version comes in an eleven-ounce wool fabric, and with its vest it is perfectly suitable for winter wear. Without the vest, it adds distinction and style to the summer wardrobe; don a mini-check pink shirt, and the somber gray pin-stripe is catapulted into summer. The tab collar ensures that the shirt will not be mistaken for anything but business wear. The black grenadine tie, a favorite of the late George Frazier, adds another sobering touch to the pink check. Its luscious texture, however, makes certain that there is no diminution of the visual image. The windowpane overplaid handkerchief fills the void of pattern left by the solid tie. Its accent colors are a final complement to the shirt, suit, and tie grounding.

Variation: For colder weather, the suit is worn with the vest and a straight-point-collar shirt with a silver pin to maintain the tonal harmony of the ensemble. The gray-and-red pin-stripe on the shirt is narrow enough that it does not compete with the striping of the suit. The two kinds of stripes are brought together by the gray, black, and red of the woven silk English macclesfield tie. The simple white handkerchief enhances the aura of dignity and purposefulness.

3. The Glen Plaid

The summer glen plaid is a cousin to the winter version, only it is made with a lightweight fabric and a lighter and more distinct pattern. If you want a plaid suit, this is the classic. First worn by the Duke of Windsor, who shocked his fellow racing enthusiasts when he showed up at the track in a double-breasted version with the unlikely pairing of brown suede shoes. The white broadcloth shirt with round eyelet collar is light and summery. The pin shown is silver, but this striped tie could easily take a gold pin as well. The wide gauge of the tie's stripings allows it to be paired with the pattern of the suit. Its summery texture draws out the tropical quality of the suit.

Variation: It used to be common to wear a more textured open-weave shirt in summer. This cotton blue voile is extremely elegant, yet it is also light and cool. The collar is an English-spread, a sophisticated collar for a sophisticated man's shirt. The tie has been knotted in a half-Windsor knot—traditional with a spread collar.

4. The Tan Gabardine

This suit is a luxury: too light for winter, too warm for summer. Yet how can one resist the luscious silky feel? It is just the right ticket for spring or fall. A campus favorite of the Ivy League in the twenties, it takes effort to find a gabardine suit ready-made today (manufacturers fear to produce it because its hard-finish fabric shows every error). Its replacement, the tan wool, is a duller, less elegant substitute. Still, this color makes an invaluable contribution to a summer wardrobe, as its neutral color allows a limitless variation of summer color and pattern. The striped English broadcloth shirt with tab collar is in tonal support of the suit. The printed blue-and-white polka dot provides a needed contrast while still reflecting the subtle blue striping of the shirt. The white dots oblige the wearer to don a fresh white handkerchief as well.

Variation: The button-down collar and mini-tattersall shirt give this outfit a slightly more casual look. The bright yellow and paisley handkerchief take advantage of summer's expanded color palette.

5. The Cotton Poplin

The cotton poplin suit is light, comfortable, and inexpensive—the perfect knockabout suit for the active businessman. This version is an olive green, a standard since the natural-shoulder phenomenon of the fifties took hold. An alternative color is beige. The rich blue color of the club-collar end-on-end cotton shirt adds a richness to the cotton poplin, which does have a tendency to look faded. With two solids, the opportunity presents itself for a boldly striped tie. The figured handkerchief balances the strength of the tie.

Variation: Red is another rich color to give added life to the olive poplin. The end-on-end striped button-down-collar shirt is strong enough to facilitate a slightly less busy tie—in this case, a handsome navy club tie. The button-down collar and the tie itself reflect the collegiate, natural-shoulder origins of the suit. The blue, green, and red silk paisley handkerchief continues the interplay among the three predominant colors of the ensemble.

6. The Oxford-Striped Seersucker

The all-American summer suit: the all-cotton striped seersucker. Originally thought of as a Southern boy's fabric, seersucker became a mainstay of the American summer wardrobe when a wealthy stockbroker discovered its comfort and wore it one day on Wall Street. Cool and deliciously crisp, putting it on feels like climbing into a bed of fresh linens. Blue-and-white constitutes the most common version, followed closely by gray, brown, and olive with white. The jacket can double as a sports jacket with a pair of gray tropical wool slacks or tan gabardine. As befits a crinkly, casual suit, it looks best with a sporty-collared shirt. The bold stripes suggest the wearing of a solid-colored shirt and a tie with a wide spatial pattern, either in a stripe or a print.

Variation: Nothing is simpler than matching a white button-down oxford shirt with a blue-and-white seersucker suit. Yet there is beauty in the simplicity and freshness. The colorful cotton madras bow tie is bright and a bit whimsical, and the white handkerchief is neither overly showy nor invisible.

7. The Summer Blazer

The summer blazer has all the virtues of its winter brother: it is stylish, versatile, and easy to accessorize. It is perhaps even more wearable, since even some of the stuffiest businesses have a slightly more relaxed sense of decorum in the face of summer's heat. The classic blue blazer is a perfect foil for bold stripings and bright patterns. Here a candy-striped English-spread-collar shirt brightens as well as dresses up this normally casual jacket. The club tie is simple but direct, and the white handkerchief uses a satin border of navy and red to reflect the regimental cast of the outfit. Turn in your briefcase and gray tropical trousers for a pair of white duck or, more elegant still, wool doeskins, and you're ready to answer any weekend invitation.

Variation: The versatility of the blazer may be its single greatest virtue. To turn it into a casual jacket, just add a button-down tattersall shirt and a bright linen tie. The solid-colored tie allows a brightly patterned handkerchief to be worn. The silk paisley is always puff-folded—a bit of sport in the breast pocket.

8. The Summer Sports Jacket

The plaid madras jacket is as all-American as the striped seersucker suit. Its colors are as rich and varied as the colors of summer, and the fabric is light and cool. There is no question about which item of clothing is the predominant player in the ensemble when you wear a madras jacket: the accessories always play a subordinate role. The dark pink end-on-end button-down shirt and green-figured tie highlight the colors of the jacket. The yellow handkerchief adds the finishing touch.

Variation: The yellow button-down shirt is the perfect mate for this most venerable of American country-club classics. The heavy patterning of the jacket requires the choice of a quiet or distant pattern in the tie. The club pattern of the silk tie adds a bit of unexpected fun: Santa Claus and skiers in the midst of summer. The red silk handkerchief brings out the colors of the jacket once again.

All the styles and suggestions given in this book are only intended to show the possibilities. It is up to each person to create his own style. That is the art—and the fun—of dressing well.

Glossary

A

acetate—a fiber produced from cellulose, acetic acid, and other chemicals.

airing—the hanging of woolen clothes in the open to revitalize the material and restore it to its original state.

air permeability—the porousness of a fabric, determining its warmth or coolness.

alpaca—the fiber from a llamalike animal, often used for insulated coats and shell-stitched sweaters.

angora—a fiber derived from the Angora goat.

antelope—antelope skin, normally of suede texture and used for shoes, belts, and so on.

apron—of a tie; the front apron of a tie is the wide end; the rear apron is the narrow end.

argyle—any multicolored knitted diamond pattern with an overplaid; primarily used in hose and sweaters.

Argyll—a county of Scotland and title held by Scottish clan of Campbell; sometimes used interchangeably with "argyle," which denotes the same pattern.

armscye—the lower side of the armhole into which the sleeve of a coat or jacket is sewn.

Art Deco—symmetrical or rectilinear geometrical design used on sweaters and other items of apparel inspired by Russian ballet, Bauhaus, Cubism, American Indian crafts, and Art Nouveau.

ascot—a double-knot tie with the ends folded over and held in place with a stickpin and used for formal day wear.

automatic wash-and-wear—any garment that may be run through wash and spin cycles of an automatic washer, then through the automatic dryer and subsequently worn with little or no ironing.

awning stripes—bold, broad stripes, in sturdy fabrics for awnings; also descriptive of bold stripes for sport shirts or jackets.

B

backless waistcoat—a waistcoat, usually for formal wear, that has been made without a back and is usually held in place by bands held together by a buckle or a button across the back of the waistline.

bal collar—a type of high military collar, approximately 3½ inches wide, found on a raincoat or overcoat, which may be worn flat or turned up and buttoned (derived from balmacaan).

balmacaan—an overcoat with raglan shoulders and narrow, turned-down collar. Named for estate called Balmacaan near Inverness, Scotland, and called "bal" for short.

Balmoral—a tartan of the British royal family, as well as a heavy woolen material in red, blue, and black plaid. Also the name given the bal shoe.

bal (balmoral) shoe—a closed-throat shoe with a lace-up front whose name is derived from the Balmoral Castle in Scotland.

bandolier cloth—a coarse woven cotton or other fabric used for belts.

Bannockburn—Scottish tweed produced by alternating two-ply and single-ply yarns in the warp and filling. The name is derived from the battle won by Scots over England in 1314 under Robert Bruce.

barathea—silk, rayon, cotton, or wool with pebble effect used primarily in neckwear and evening wear.

barleycorn—a design of miniature proportions primarily used for tweeds and other woolens.

barrel cuff—a single cuff attached to a shirt sleeve with buttonhole closure.

Barrymore collar—a low-set attached collar with long points. First worn by the actor John Barrymore, but later popular among others in California, thus sometimes referred to as the "California collar."

bar-shaped tie—a four-in-hand tie whose ends are parallel and of equal width.

bar tack—a series of overstitches used to close back of quality tie.

basket weave—used primarily in shirtings, this is a variation on plain-weave fabric in which several yarns are worked in warp and weft.

batik—Indonesian method of dying fabrics wherein waxed areas resist dye, leaving colors to unwaxed areas.

batiste—a thin finely woven fabric of cotton or other fibers named for Baptiste of Damrai, a French weaver of fine linen, and generally used for shirts and underwear.

battle jacket—a single-breasted waist-length khaki woolen World War II regulation army jacket.

batwing—a square-shaped bow tie in ribbed silk, velvet, or satin for evening wear, or in a patterned fabric for business or casual wear.

beaver cloth—fabric of double-thickness woven wool with a smooth, long fiber surface, usually used in overcoats.

Bedford cord—a ribbed weave, closely woven, sturdy fabric with raised cord effect in wool, cotton, silk, acrylic, or polyester fibers or other blends.

beer jacket—a white denim jacket traditionally worn by male members of senior class at Princeton in the spring. The design changes each year, and a numeral appears on the back of the jacket.

bell-bottoms—trousers flared at the bottom so as to suggest the shape of a bell.

bellows pleat—a deep fold at the side of a garment to provide fullness for comfort.

bellows pocket—a pocket with pleats to allow for expansion.

bench-made—shoes strictly handmade by one craftsman; also refers to shoes featuring hand-sewn soles.

bengaline—a ribbed fabric of silk, worsted, or worsted blends used in men's suits and trousers.

Bengal stripes—colorful striped fabric from Bengal, India, used primarily for beachwear, sports shirts, pajamas, and neckwear.

beret—a felt or fabric round-crown cap without a brim in a solid color.

Bermuda shorts—walking shorts of a style worn in Bermuda, extending to approximately the break at the knee.

besom—a jacket or coat pocket with a stitched fold on the upper and lower sides.

bespoke—an English term meaning custom-made.

bias—a 45-degree diagonal line on the fabric.

bikini—abbreviated swim shorts also used in men's underwear.

billiard cloth—a heavyweight wool fabric with a smooth, even surface.

billycock—the British term for a derby or bowler hat, named for its inventor, Bill Coke.

bird's-eye—a woven or knitted two- or three-color small pattern for suiting, neckwear, or hosiery with a small dot resembling a bird's eye.

bi-swing jacket—a sports jacket with a gusset extending from the shoulder to the waistline of both sides, usually with a stitched-on half-belt in back.

blade—fullness of fabric above the shoulder blades of a jacket, originating with the custom tailors of London.

blazer—a single- or double-breasted sports jacket with metal buttons, either in dark blue or other solid color or stripes.

bleeding—occurs when the dye in a fabric is not fast and runs when wet.

blucher—originally a military boot named for Field Marshal Gebhard Leberecht von Blücher of the Prussian Army, it is open-laced in front over the instep; now a low shoe with a similar open-throat front.

boat neck—a horizontal opening at the neck of a pullover.

bold look—a complete outfit look of 1948, which included neckwear with large dots, broad stripes of strong checks, a shirt with spread collar, a hat with wide binding at the edge of the brim, and positive-design socks and bulky shoes.

bomber jacket—a U.S. Air Force pilot's waist-length jacket of leather with sheepskin lining.

breeches—knee-length trousers.

British warmer—a military-design double-breasted overcoat in knee or slightly above knee length that is shaped at the body and slightly flared toward the bottom.

broadcloth—a fabric that is closely woven with the rib running weftwise; it is often made of lustrous cotton, polyester and cotton, all polyester, or other fibers.

brocade—a rich jacquard-woven fabric with an all-over interwoven design of raised flowers. Derived from the Spanish word *brocado*, meaning "to ornament."

brogue—a rough, heavy shoe of untanned leather with a thong closure, from the Scottish Highlands and Ireland; now an oxford shoe with perforations at the toe and seams at the border.

Brummell, Beau (George Bryan)—a dandy of early nineteenth-century England (1778–1840).

buckskin—a velvet-finish leather derived from deer and elk, which has been buffed; used in gloves, shoes, and so on.

bunting—lightweight closely woven wool or cotton used for banners and sports shirts.

bush jacket—a single-breasted belted shirt jacket with four flap pockets, also known as a safari jacket.

bushwing—a clothing alteration.

butterfly tie—a bow tie with flared ends, primarily used for evening wear.

button-down collar—a collar held down at the points by buttons, first used in nineteenth-century England by polo players to keep their shirt collars from flapping in the wind.

button-through—a closure on a jacket or coat with buttonholes cut through the entire nap of fabric.

boot jack—a woven frame in shape of a **V** or **U** which holds the boot while it is being removed from the foot.

boot tree—a wooden or metal form put in a boot to hold its shape when it is not being worn.

boutonniere—a flower worn in the lapel of a jacket or overcoat.

box pleat—a pleat with edges folded in opposite directions; used on jackets and shirts.

braces—English synonym for suspenders.

braid—a narrow ribbon of fabric used on side seam of dress trousers, robes, hat, and so on.

break—a crease or fold across the vamp of a shoe, or the crease of the trousers over the instep of a shoe.

C

cable stitch—an overlapping knit stitch simulating a cable, used primarily in sweaters and hose.

calfskin—soft, tanned skin of calf used in footwear and other leather goods.

calico—an old term for a plain-woven printed cotton cloth.

cambric—a closely woven cotton fabric resembling linen.

camel's hair—a fabric of soft, woollike texture; varies in color from light tan to brownish black. Used alone or combined with wool in coats, suits, sweaters, and sportswear.

canvas—a coarsely woven cotton or linen fabric.

capote—a hooded coat or cloak; also a military overcoat.

carat—a unit of weight used for precious metals.

cardigan—named for the 7th Earl of Cardigan, leader of the Charge of the Light Brigade in the Crimean War, this is a knitted sweater without a collar or lapels, with a button through the front or a kind of knit stitch.

Carnaby Street—a two-block-long street in London where several shops introduced the "mod" look of clothing in the 1960s.

casein—a fiber derived from milk and blended with wool, cotton, mohair, and rayon for knitting or weaving into fabrics used for buttons.

cashmere—a fine grade of wool from the long-haired Kashmir goat, woven into soft fabrics for use in coats, sweaters, and other articles of clothing.

cavalry twill—a sturdy-weave fabric.

chalk stripes—stripes resembling chalk lines; used primarily in men's suits.

challis—a napped fabric of lightweight worsted wool, spun rayon, or blends, usually with printed figures on it; used in neckwear.

chambray—a fabric woven with colored warp and white filling, resulting in a frosted colored surface; made in cotton or spun rayon with a small plain-weave effect; it is used for shirts, sportswear, and pajamas.

chamois—tanned skin from the European chamois goat or from a sheep or lamb; used primarily for jackets, gloves, and sportswear accessories.

change pocket—a small pocket with or without a flap, placed above the right-hand lower pocket of a jacket or coat.

Charvet—a reverse repp fabric with a double-ridge effect. Originally called Gegence, but the name is now associated with the firm of Charvet et Fils.

Chesterfield—named for the nineteenth-century Earl of Chesterfield, this is a beltless, semi-fitted single- or double-breasted overcoat for town wear that may have a velvet collar. Those who wished to express disapproval of the executions during the French Revolution added black velvet collars to their coats as a sign of mourning. It has since become a mark of fashion.

cheviot—originally a wool fabric from fibers of sheep grown in the Cheviot hills on border between England and Scotland; now a rough wool fabric or blends of fibers in herringbone or twill weave.

chevron weave—a vertical zigzag broken twill similar to a herringbone.

chino cloth—an all-cotton twill used in military uniforms, as well as a cotton and polyester blend used in trousers and other sportswear; usually khaki colored.

chukka—an ankle-high boot in suede or smooth leather that has two eyelets, with rubber or leather soles.

clear-face or finished worsted—a fabric of tightly twisted worsted yarns; it is closely sheared and scoured to show the weave.

clock—an up-and-down knitted or embroidered design on the side of hose.

club bow tie—a straight-cut tie for evening wear, with a generous center knot; it is white when worn with a tailcoat, black or midnight blue when worn with a dinner jacket.

combing—a process that produces even, compact, fine, smooth yarn by eliminating short fibers and arranging the yarn in parallel lines.

Continental Look—a suit with a short, shaped, side-vented jacket and tapered, cuffless trousers.

cord—a fabric with a raised rib effect.

cordovan—originally a long-wearing leather with a waxy finish from Córdoba, Spain, the term is now descriptive of men's accessories in a dark burgundy shade and made from a horse's rump.

corduroy—a plain- or twill-weave fabric of polyester, cotton, rayon, or blends with a cut-pile surface of wide or narrow wales.

counter—the back portion of a shoe above the heel.

covert—a woolen twill fabric that has been tightly woven and made from two yarns of different shades, resulting in a mixed effect.

cravat—a term sometimes used to designate better neckwear; also a tie that is wrapped around the neck without knotting.

crepe—a crinkled-surface fabric made of silk, cotton, polyester, wool, or blends.

crew neck—a collarless opening that follows the contour of the neck on beach, Basque, or pullover shirts, sweaters, or underwear.

cummerbund—a waistband of solid color or patterned silk, rayon, cotton, or polyester, with or without pleats, to be worn with a dinner jacket.

cutaway—a formal coat with tails that extend to the break of the knees in the rear with one button; it is single-breasted in front, with peaked lapels.

D

dart—a tuck taken in to fit a garment to the body.

demibosòm—the short, starched plain or pleated bosom of a shirt.

denim—a twill-weave fabric in cotton or a blend of fibers. Extremely sturdy, this fabric was first produced in eighteenth-century Nîmes, France—hence its name, which is a corruption of "de Nîmes."

derby—a hard-finish hat of felt, with a rounded crown and stiff, curled-edge brim; also called a bowler.

dimple—the crease formed in the center of a tie just below the knot when the knot has been properly tied.

dinner jacket—an evening jacket for semi-formal or formal wear. Worn with matching or black dress trousers, it may be single- or double-breasted in black, white, or colored fabric, with peaked lapels or shawl collar.

doeskin—the suede side of the skin of a doe, sheep, or lamb.

dolman sleeve—a full-cut sleeve that is very wide at the armhole.

Donegal tweed—a woolen tweed originally from County Donegal, Ireland, characterized by colorful nubs.

double-breasted—a kind of jacket, waistcoat, or outercoat in which the fabric overlaps a few inches in the front.

double-knit—a double-faced material knitted with solid colors on both sides or with a pattern on one side.

double-soled—a shoe or boot with extra thickness on the soles.

drape—the way in which the fabric of a garment hangs from the shoulders or the waist.

drip-dry—a fabric that dries quickly without spinning, wringing, or squeezing the garment.

duck—a plain, closely woven fabric of cotton or other blends that resembles light-weight canvas.

dungaree—originally, a coarse twill cotton made in Bombay; today, it refers to work slacks or jeans in blue denim.

E

Edwardian—fashions favored by Edward VII of England around the turn of this century.

end-and-end—a weave with alternate warp yarns of white and color, forming fine checks.

English drape—a single- or double-breasted jacket style with fullness about the chest, forming wrinkles and added fullness over the shoulder blades; also called the lounge suit.

espadrille—a rope-soled beach and sports sandal with canvas uppers, originated by Spanish and French dock hands.

eyelet—a small hole made to hold a lace, such as in shoes or in a shirt collar to hold a bar.

F

faille—a rib-weave fabric with a cord effect.

Fair Isle sweater—a colorfully designed horizontal-patterned knit sweater from Fair Isle, off the coast of Scotland, that was originally made by hand.

fast—a term describing colors that retain their original shade after washing, exposure to sunlight, and other elements.

fedora—a soft felt hat with a center crease and rolled brim, named for the Victorien Sardou melodrama of 1882, *Fédora*, written especially for Sarah Bernhardt.

felt—a material produced from animal fibers through moisture, steam, and pressure.

finishing—the treatment of a fabric by covering its surface to improve its appearance.

flannel—a loosely woven fabric with a napped surface that hides the weave; it is primarily made of wool or cotton.

flax—plant fibers that are the source of linen.

flocking—a surface finish or design produced by spraying short fibers so that they adhere electrostatically to a material.

fly front—a closure in which a placket or piece of fabric covers the buttons or zippers.

fob—a chain connecting a pocket to a watch or key chain or the ornament attached to such a chain.

fold collar—a double shirt collar of turn-down style, attached or separate.

foulard—a soft, lightweight tie fabric, often made of silk, rayon, or acetate, with a plain or twilled surface printed with a small, evenly spaced pattern.

four-in-hand—a tie, usually 52 to 58 inches in length, consisting of a large end, neckband, and short end; also a type of knot used by carriage drivers in eighteenth-century England.

French cuff—a turned back or double-cuff of a shirt that is fastened with cufflinks.

full-fashioned—a flat-knit process, characterized by the addition and reduction of stitches in order to shape the fabric to conform to body lines when seamed.

fused collar—a collar that is stiffened by the insertion of an interlining, enabling the outer fabric to be laminated through heat and pressure.

G

gabardine—a tightly woven worsted cotton, rayon, or blended fabric showing a steep twill. May be made of single- or double-ply yarns.

galluses—an archaic name for suspenders.

galosh—a rubber rain overshoe closed in front by a zipper or by buckles.

gauge—a standard of the measure of thickness or fineness of a knitted fabric, dependent upon the number of needles used in given unit of space.

gauntlet—a long glove flared from the wrist to the middle portion of the forearm; also the English term for the sleeve placket, the open area just before the cuff.

gillie—a tongueless oxford that laces across the instep and ties around the ankle.

gingham—a plain-weave fabric of cotton in checks, stripes, or plaids.

glenurquhart—a Scottish clan plaid with an overplaid in another shade or color formed by groups of lines crossing at right angles to form a boxlike design; used for suitings and for sportswear.

gorge—the line where the collar and the lapel meet.

gray goods—fabric as it comes from the loom before being treated.

grenadine—a gauzelike neckwear fabric in which threads cross one another from side to side.

grosgrain—a fabric of silk, rayon, or other fibers along with a cotton filling so as to produce a ribbed effect.

guard's coat—a long, dark-colored overcoat with a half-belt inverted center pleat and deep folds at the sides.

gun-club check—an even check pattern with alternating rows of color.

gusset—a fabric section inserted at the seam of a garment to allow extra fullness and to serve as a reinforcement.

H

hacking jacket—a riding coat, longer than a regular sports coat, with a slight flare at the bottom, a deep side or center vent, slanting pockets, and a change pocket on the right side above the lower pocket.

hair cloth—a wiry cotton fabric made with horsehair or mohair filling and used for stiffening.

hairline stripe—a striped design woven in one-thread thickness in worsteds and other fabrics.

hand-blocked—a description of material printed by hand with a wooden or wood-and-metal block.

hand-rolled hem—the edge of a handkerchief or other accessory rolled and stitched by hand.

handwoven—fabrics woven on a loom operated by the hand and foot.

hank—a unit of measure of yarn or thread.

Harris tweed—a woolen material spun, dyed, and woven by hand by crofters of Harris and Lewis and other Outer Hebrides islands.

heat-setting—the application of heat and pressure to a fabric so that it holds its crease.

hem—the finish produced by turning back the raw edge of a material and sewing it by hand or machine.

herringbone—a ribbed, twilled fabric in which equal numbers of threads slant right and left forming a chevron pattern.

high-count fabric—tightly woven material.

high-water pants—trousers that reach only slightly above the ankles.

homburg—a soft felt hat with a stiff, curled brim and tapered crown; worn in black or midnight blue with a dinner jacket for semi-formal wear, and in other colors for day wear. Originated in German resort town of Homburg.

homespun—a loose-weave material first produced by hand and later by machine.

houndstooth check—a check with uneven edges, resembling teeth of a dog.

hunter's pink—the traditional bright scarlet coat color of formal hunting garb.

I

Icelandic wool—wool from Icelandic sheep that is long and glossy as well as the most water-repellent and wind-resistant fiber in existence.

indigo—the plant source used for blue dye for fabrics prior to the development of coal-tar dyes.

inseam—the distance from the crotch to the bottom of the trousers.

insole—the portion of the shoe between the welt and the outer sole.

intarsia—a knitted design motif giving the effect of having been inlaid in the fabric. The name is derived from the Italian *intarsiare*, meaning "to inlay."

inverted pleat—a pleat with fullness on the inside (the reverse of a box pleat).

Irish linen—a thin linen woven from Irish flax.

Irish poplin—a silk-and-wool material used in men's neckwear.

Ivy League—a description of a suit in which the jacket has natural shoulders, hangs straight, and has a center vent. The trousers are plain-front and hang straight. This name is registered by Botany Industries.

J

jacquard—a type of knitting that produces all-over or sectional designs of color and texture in a fabric.

jazz suit—a suit popular in the 1920s that was characterized by a narrow-shoulder jacket having a wasp-waist plain or pinched back with a deep center vent and flared lines; one, two, or three buttons; and trousers that were peg-legged.

jerkin—a tight-fitting jacket or waistcoat with button or zipper closure.

jersey—a knitted fabric with a slight rib on one side; the name is derived from the Island of Jersey, where sailors first wore sweaters made of this fabric.

jivy Ivy—a description of an ensemble of a narrow-shouldered jacket with a four-button single-breasted front and tight-fitting trousers.

jodhpurs—riding trousers that are flared at the hips and narrow from the knee to the ankle and finished with or without cuffs.

K

khaki—Hindi word meaning "dust-colored." It is a neutral color.

kid—a soft leather made from the skin of a mature goat or young goat.

kipper—an English term for a wide necktie that looks like a salmon or herring.

knickers—also called knickerbockers, they are loose trousers draped over the knees and fastened with a band and buckle above the calf; originally worn for golf, they are made of tweed, gabardine, flannel, and washable fabrics. The name is derived from Dietrich Knickerbocker, the fictional author of "A History of New York" (1809) by Washington Irving.

L

lambswool—the first shearing of wool from lambs seven to nine months old. It is somewhat finer and softer than wool from mature sheep.

lapel—the portion of the front of a jacket or coat that is turned back on both sides of the opening from the collar downward.

last—a wood or metal form shaped like a foot upon which a shoe is fashioned.

line—the style or outline of a garment.

linen—a fabric produced from flax fibers and one of the oldest textiles, dating back to ancient Egypt.

lisle—a fabric of fine, hard-twisted, long-staple cotton thread, of two or more ply yarns.

Loafer—a moccasin-style shoe. This slip-on shoe is a brand name registered by Nettleton Shops, Inc.

loden—a fleecy water-repellent coating utilizing greasy wool. It was first produced in the Tyrolean Alps.

loden coat—a coat of loden cloth, double-breasted, with a yoke front and back and a wooden toggle-type closure.

loft—a term describing the resiliency or spring of a fabric after it has been put under pressure.

long-roll collar—a low-front collar on shirts that have 3¾- to 4-inch points.

lounge suit—*see* English drape.

lovat—a heather mixture of full blue or dull green combined with tan or gray. It describes the color obtained by this mixture, not a particular fabric.

luster—the sheen or reflecting quality of a fabric.

M

macclesfield—a small, neat all-over pattern generally made with a dobby loom. The name is derived from the Macclesfield parish in England, where the Huguenot weavers settled after being expelled from France.

mackinaw—a kind of heavy, napped wool blanket in large stripes or checks. It received its name from Old Mackinac, Michigan, around which it was used in bartering with the Indians.

madder—a Eurasian plant root from which a dye stuff was derived.

madras—plain-weave cotton or blended fabrics in stripes or checks which were named for Madras, India, an early textile source.

marl—a two-tone yarn that produces a heatherlike mixture in fabric.

matte finish—a dull finish.

medallion—a perforated design in the tip of a leather shoe.

melton—a compact, heavily felted woolen fabric, usually of plain weave with a short-napped surface.

mercerized cotton—named for John Mercer, an English calico printer. Mercerizing, which he invented in 1844, is a process that treats cotton and other fabrics so that they become smooth and lustrous; it also improves dye penetration.

merino—wool from the Australian merino sheep that is woven into a soft fabric resembling cashmere.

mess jacket—a semi-formal white waist-length military jacket that has been adapted for civilian wear.

moccasin—a slip-on shoe adapted from the Indian shoe made from one piece of leather sewn over a vamp.

mohair—the fleece of the Angora goat, characterized by a soft and silky texture and rich luster.

moiré—a wavy pattern on a ribbed fabric that is produced by crushing the ribs with an engraved roller.

moleskin cloth—a cotton-filled sateen fabric backed with a thick nap resembling fur.

momme—a Japanese unit of weight used in the silk industry.

monk-front shoe—a shoe with a plain tip and buckle and strap above the instep.

mules—counterless house slippers.

muslin—a firm cotton cloth with a plain weave, it is one of oldest staple cotton cloths.

N

nailhead—a small, dotted design used for sharkskin worsteds.

napping—a finishing process to raise the fibers of a cloth to the surface by means of revolving cylinders.

natural shoulders—a design in which a minimum of padding is contained in the shoulder, such as in the cut of a natural-shoulder suit. Also a term for such a suit.

neckband shirt—a standard type of shirt finished with buttonholes in the front and back of the neckband and worn with a separate collar.

Norfolk jacket—named for the Duke of Norfolk and characterized by a box pleat in front, two similar pleats in back, and an all-around belt.

notched lapel—a fairly wide V-shaped opening at the outside edge of the seam between the collar and the lapel.

nub—a knot or tangle in yarn that gives an irregular texture to fabric.

nutria—a beaverlike fur.

nylon—a strong, washable, elastic synthetic fiber.

O

odd waistcoat—a waistcoat that, due to the pattern, material, or color, does not match the suit or jacket with which it is worn.

oilskin—a waterproof cotton raincoat processed with several coatings of oil.

ombre—a fashion term for shaded or graduated color that creates a striped effect.

opera hat—a dull silk or rayon collapsible hat with a curled brim for formal or semi-formal evening wear.

optimo—the shape of a Panama or straw hat that has a full crown and a ridge extending round the hat from back to front.

overplaid—a double-plaid cloth in which the weave or color effect is arranged in blocks of different sizes, one over the other.

oxford—a low lace-up shoe produced in blucher, gillie, and bal styles; a very dark shade of gray used for fabrics; a plain- or basket-weave cotton or cotton-and-polyester-blend shirting.

oxford bags—full-cut worsted or flannel trousers worn in the 1920s and named for Oxford University, where they were first worn.

oxford shirting—a modified plain- or basket-weave cotton fabric that originated in Oxford, England.

P

paisley—printed woven designs found in Cashmerian shawls that have been adapted to neckwear, mufflers, and sportswear.

Palm Beach cloth—a trade name for summer suiting (trademark of the Palm Beach Company).

Panama—a straw hat first brought to this country by sailors arriving back from Panama. It originated in Colombia, Peru, and Ecuador and is produced from fibers of the jipijapa plant.

parka—a hooded garment with sleeves, usually made in water-repellent fabrics for outdoor winter wear.

patch pocket—a pocket made by stitching a piece of material on the outside of a garment, with or without a flap.

Peacock Revolution—the name given to the fashion trend in the 1960s characterized by exotic colors, especially in shirts and neckwear.

peaked lapel—a lapel of a jacket or coat that comes to a point at the outer edge, with narrow spacing between the lapel and the bottom of the collar.

peau de soie—a heavyweight soft satin with a fine cross-rib.

peg-top trousers—full-cut trousers that fit wide over the hips, tapering to narrow bottoms.

pigskin—a coarse pebble-grained leather with dark bristle pits.

pile—cut or uncut loops forming the surface of a fabric that can be made in variations of twill, raised-nap, or plain-weave.

pilling—small tangles or balls on the surface of a fabric.

pima—a kind of cotton grown in the Southwest, named for Pima County, Arizona.

pin check—an end-and-end weave fabric with a fine check made with alternating colored yarns that are usually woven.

pinned rounded collar—a collar with short rounded points held in place with a pin or collar bar.

pinstripes—very fine stripes, usually in white or gray.

pinwale—corduroy material with narrow ribs or wales.

piping—narrow cord, braid, or fold used to finish or decorate the edges or pockets of a garment.

piqué—a cotton, polyester and cotton, rayon, or silk fabric with ribs running vertically, sometimes forming a honeycomb- or waffle-weave, usually used in shirts for formal wear.

placket—the piece of material on the front of the shirt where the buttonholes are placed.

plaid—a boxlike design formed by stripes running vertically and horizontally and usually associated with the Scottish tartan.

plain-weave—a weave in which the filling yarns pass over one warp yarn and under the next, alternating across each row.

plaiting—the interweaving of fibers.

pleat—a fold of material pressed or stitched so that it is held in place.

pleated bosom—a shirt bosom formed by folds usually running vertically, primarily used for formal wear.

plus fours—knickers extending four inches below the break of the knee.

ply—a measurement of yarns formed by twisting together more than one single strand.

polo coat—a double- or single-breasted overcoat of camel's hair or soft fleece with set-in or raglan sleeves, patch pockets with flaps, and a half or full belt around the waist. It was first popularized by polo players in the 1920s.

polo shirt—a knitted pullover shirt with an attached collar and front-buttoned placket first worn by polo players around the turn of the century.

polyester—a generic term for a fiber that is a condensation of polymer obtained from ethylene glycol and terephthalic acid.

pongee—a rough-woven, thin, natural-colored silk fabric.

poplin—a strong, medium-weight, plain-woven fabric with fine crosswise ribs and made of cotton, silk, wool, blends, or man-made fibers.

porkpie hat—a felt or fabric hat with a flat-topped crown that resembles an English pastry pie.

postboy waistcoat—a waistcoat originally worn by postillions on horse-drawn carriages and characterized by a five-button single-breasted front and by flap pockets on both sides.

Prince Albert—a double-breasted knee-length or longer black or dark gray frock coat named for Prince Albert Edward (later Edward VII of England), worn with striped or matching trousers for formal day wear.

pullover—a long-sleeved or sleeveless sweater or shirt with a neck opening to be pulled over the head.

pump—a low-cut slip-on shoe with a ribbed ribbon bow in front used for formal wear; may be patent leather or in a dull matte finish.

purl—a knit stitch that produces horizontal ridges on both sides of the fabric.

R

raglan—named for the first Baron Raglan, commander of British troops during the Crimean War, this is a loose-fitting coat with full-cut sleeves and a seam that extends from each armhole to the collar in both the front and the rear.

ramie—a bast fiber obtained from an eastern Asian and southern U.S. plant.

rayon—the generic term for a manufactured textile fiber or yarn produced chemically from regenerated cellulose and containing an amount of non-regenerated cellulose fiber-forming material.

ready-to-wear—a term referring to ready-made apparel.

reefer—a short single- or double-breasted fitted and tailored overcoat.

regimental stripes—authentic colors and striping patterns of British Army regiments.

repp—also spelled rep; a closely woven ribbed fabric with a transverse cord effect.

reprocessed wool—wool that has been fabricated but not worn and has been unraveled, restored to fiber, spun, and rewoven into material.

resilience—the ability of fiber or fabric to return to its original shape after having been put under pressure.

resilient construction—a method of manufacturing in which the bias-cut shell and the bias-cut interlining of a tie are held together by a resilient slip stitch so that the finished tie stretches and recovers when knotted. It was invented by Joss Langsdorf.

reverse pleat—a pleat located at the waistband of trousers that faces outward instead of inward.

rib—the cords or ridges in a woven fabric.

rise—the distance from the crotch to the top of the waistband of trousers.

roller printing—the application of designs on fabrics using engraved metal rollers.

S

sack suit—a loose-fitting single- or double-breasted suit jacket of flannel, cheviot, worsted, tweed, or other fabric.

saddle oxford—a lace-up shoe with a strip of leather over the instep in the same or different color.

Sanforized—the brand name for a process that controls fabric shrinkage.

satin—a smooth, lustrous, heavy tie fabric of silk, polyester, or other fibers.

Savile Row—a street in the West End of London where many custom tailors are located.

saxony—a lightweight fabric with a slightly napped surface.

Scotch grain—a type of leather with a deeply embossed, pebbled surface.

scouring—freeing wool of dirt, natural grease, or dried perspiration.

Sea Island—a variety of cotton grown on islands off the coast of Florida, South Carolina, and Georgia, as well as in the West Indies.

seam—a place on a garment where two pieces of material are sewn together.

seconds—lower-standard fabrics or garments.

seersucker—a lightweight fabric, usually of cotton or cotton and man-made blends, it is characterized by a crinkled, puckered surface, and is especially popular for summer garments.

sennit—also called a boater or sailor, it is a stiff straw hat with a flat oval crown and flat brim.

serge—a twill-weave, smooth-surfaced material with diagonal ribs on both sides.

set-in sleeve—a coat, shirt, or other garment sleeve that is sewn in at the armhole.

sevenfold tie—an unlined necktie made from seven folds of fabric (usually silk); this is the original method of making a tie.

sharkskin—a smooth-finished, clear-faced, twill-weave fabric made in two tones; used in worsted for suits and coats, silk for neckwear.

shawl collar—a collar extending from the waist around the neck and rolled back without notches or peaks; used on formal evening jackets.

shepherd's check—a twill-weave fabric with small even checks in contrasting colors.

Shetland—a medium-textured wool originating from a breed of sheep on the Shetland Isles. Today the term is generally applied to type of wool yarn producing a similar surface.

shoe tree—a metal or wood form used to help a shoe retain its shape when it is not being worn.

silhouette—the outline of a garment.

silk—the fiber produced by a silkworm in forming a cocoon. It is resilient and wrinkle-resistant when woven into a fabric.

silk hat—also known as a top hat, it is a stiff high-crowned formal hat made of silk plush with a stiff rolled-edge brim.

single-breasted—a jacket, waistcoat, or overcoat with a single set of buttons on one side and buttonholes on the other.

single cuff—a shirt cuff fastened either with buttons or cufflinks.

skimmer—a sennit straw hat.

slash pocket—a pocket set into a slash opening either vertically or at an angle.

slicker—a raincoat of oiled cotton or silk.

slip stitching—a method of sewing in which the shell and interlining of a tie are joined together by a special stitch that permits the tie to stretch and recover.

slub—a tangle in the yarn, either by design or accident, that gives fabric a rough texture.

smoking jacket—a jacket of wool, brocade, velvet, silk, or blend that is worn indoors for leisure wear.

snap-brim hat—any hat with a brim designed to be turned down in front or on the side and up in the rear.

spats—from the word "spatterdashes," these are ankle coverings fastened at the sides with buckles or buttons and held under the shoe with straps and buckles.

staple—a term describing the average length of any fiber.

starched bosom—a set-in shirt front of two or more fabric thicknesses with a stiff, smooth surface and intended to be worn with formal wear.

stud—a pin or button fastener for the bosom of a shirt worn for formal occasions. The stud may be made of colored stone, tooled or plain metal, pearl, or enamel.

suede—leather of which the flesh side is buffed to a smooth finish. The word is derived from the French *suede*, meaning "Sweden," where the process originated.

support socks—hose made with stretch yarn or vertical and horizontal ribbing in order to provide support for the calf.

suspenders—two straps or bands worn over the shoulders and across the back, then attached to the trousers for support.

T

tab—a piece of fabric with a buttonhole for fastening a button on the opposite side.

tab collar—a shirt collar held together by use of tabs.

tailcoat—an evening coat with tails beginning at the waist seam, extending to the side seams, and tapering in the back to the bend of the knee. The coat extends to the waist in the front and does not button. Lapels have grosgrain or satin facing in midnight blue or black. A tailcoat is formal evening wear and is to be worn with white tie only.

tartan—a plaid design associated with a specific Scottish clan.

tattersall—named for the horsemarket originated in London in 1766 by Richard Tattersall, it is a checked pattern of vertical and horizontal stripes in one or two colors on a light-colored background.

tensile strength—the pressure a fabric can withstand without breaking.

textile—any knitted, woven, or felted fabric.

thistle-shaped bow tie—a straight, narrow bow tie.

three-by-six rib—six ribs of knitting on outside of fabric separated by three ribs on the reverse side.

ticket pocket—a small pocket on the right-hand side of a jacket or overcoat directly above the regular pocket.

tie bar—a clip, chain, or pin used to hold a necktie to the placket of a shirt.

tie clasp—a clam or slip-on metal holder used to keep a tie in place.

toe box—a piece of leather found inside the tip of a shoe that maintains the shoe's shape.

tongue—a strip of leather attached to the top of the vamp on the inside of a shoe under the laces as protection.

topper—an alternative name for a top hat.

town suit—a suit especially for business wear.

trench coat—a double-breasted overcoat patterned after the gabardine coat worn by British Army officers in the trenches during World War I.

tricot—a thin, lightweight fabric of single-ply or fine yarn.

trilby hat—derived from the nineteenth-century novel *Trilby*, this is a felt hat with a rolled brim that was first worn in England.

tuck—a small fold sewn into a garment.

tuxedo—a dinner jacket.

TV fold—a manner of folding a handkerchief so that one-half inch appears above the pocket line of a suit.

tweed—any rough-textured, varied-pattern woolen fabric first woven by crofters near the Tweed River in Scotland; its name is derived from *tweel* or *tweed*, the Scottish word for "twill."

twist—a turn of the ply or thread in yarn for fabric manufacture.

Tyrolean hat—a hat associated with the Austrian Tyrol that has a sharply tapered crown, narrow brim turned up in the rear and down in front, and a cord band decorated with a brush or feather.

U

Ulster—a long double-breasted overcoat with a large convertible collar, wide lapels, and a half or full belt around the waist.

unconstructed suit—a business or casual suit made without padding or lining and sometimes of double-faced material.

unfinished worsted—a fabric of medium-twisted worsted yarn; its twill weave is concealed by a slightly napped surface.

union suit—underwear of shirt and shorts or trousers in one piece.

V

vamp—the upper part of a shoe that extends forward to the toe cap and part or all the way to the rear seam.

velvet—a fabric featuring a soft, thick, short-pile surface of silk or rayon with a cotton back, or such a fabric of all silk or all cotton.

venetian cloth—a cotton or wool fabric that is warp-faced and smooth-textured.

vest—*see* waistcoat.

vicuña—a soft fabric made from the wool of the vicuña, a llamalike animal; considered the finest wool.

virgin wool—natural wool that is being used for the first time in a fabric.

Viyella—registered name of a wool-and-cotton blend in woven or knitted fabrics.

voile—a sheer cotton fabric.

W

waistband—the band around the waist at the top of trousers or shorts.

waistcoat—also known as a vest, it is a single- or double-breasted sleeveless coat of waist length, fastened by buttons or a zipper and usually worn under a jacket.

warp—also known as an end, it is a yarn running lengthwise on a loom, under tension as the fabric is being woven.

waterproofing—a process that makes a material resistant to water by closing the openings of the fabric.

wear testing—testing a fabric for strength, resiliency, flexibility, washing, creasing, and so on, based on the wearing of the garment.

weaving—a method of producing a fabric on a loom by interlacing warp and filling threads with one another.

weft—yarn running crosswise in fabric. It is also a synonym for filling yarn.

weighted silk—silk made heavier by adding a metallic solution, giving it a rich appearance.

Wellington boot—a high waterproof boot.

welt—the narrow strip of leather attached to the upper and the edge of the insole of a shoe.

welt edge—the edge of a hat brim that can be either turned back and stitched or felted by a special process.

whipcord—a coarse twill-weave fabric made of hand-twisted yarns.

widespread collar—a collar with wide difference between the points.

Windsor, Duke of (earlier Prince of Wales, briefly King Edward VIII; 1894–1972)—a member of the British royal family who exerted tremendous fashion influence from the twenties to the forties of this century and is credited with many fashion innovations, from the tab collar, snap-brim hat, and Fair Isle sweater to the Windsor knot.

Windsor collar—a collar with a wide spread between the points to accommodate the wide Windsor knot.

wing collar—a stand-up band collar with folded-back tabs or wings, worn mostly for formal wear.

wing-tip shoe—a shoe with the tip in the shape of the spread wing of a bird, with perforated seams and toe-cap design.

woolen yarn—a soft, bulky, and lofty yarn of intermixed short fibers of various length that has been crisscrossed randomly, allowing the fibers to open up and develop a very soft "cover" finish.

worsted—a smooth, firm, and compact yarn spun from combed long-staple wool fibers.

woven—a class of fabric in which the pattern is part of the weave, as opposed to prints, embroideries, and hand paints, in which the pattern is applied after the fabric is woven.

Y

yarn—fibers spun into a continuous strand.

yarn-dyed—yarns that have been dyed before having been woven or knitted.

yoke—fabric fitted over the shoulders and joined to the lower part of a garment by a seam across the chest or rear.

Z

zoot suit—worn by some men during the period between 1939 and 1942, it was characterized by a jacket with heavily padded shoulders and tapered waist that extended to a few inches above the knees. The trousers were cut full and tapered at the bottom. Supposedly derived from a suit drawn by Al Capp for his cartoon character, L'il Abner.

About the Author

Alan Flusser is a 1983 Coty Award-winning menswear designer and a 1985 nominee for the Cutty Sark Award for outstanding U.S. menswear designer. In addition, he is the author of a previous book on fashion, *Making the Man*, and has written numerous articles on men's clothes and style for such publications as *The New York Times* and *Gentlemen's Quarterly*, among others. He has been elected to the International Best-Dressed List. Mr. Flusser lives in New York City with his wife, Marilise, and their two daughters.

INDEX